AQA

AS LEVEL
MUSIC

Revision
Guide

RICHARD BRISTOW &
RICHARD KNIGHT

RHINEGOLD
EDUCATION

First published 2017 in Great Britain by
Rhinegold Education
14-15 Berners Street
London W1T 3LJ, UK
www.rhinegoldeducation.co.uk

You should always check the current
requirements of your examination,
since these may change.

Editors: Sarah Lambie and Katharine Allenby
Cover and book design: Fresh Lemon Australia

AQA AS Level Music Revision Guide
Order no. RHG142
ISBN 978-1-78558-157-1

Exclusive Distributors:
Music Sales Ltd
Distribution Centre, Newmarket Road
Bury St Edmunds, Suffolk IP33 3YB, UK

Printed in the EU

Available from Rhinegold Education for your course:

- **AQA AS and A Level Music Study Guide**
- **AQA AS and A Level Music Listening Tests**

You may find the following books useful too:

- **AS Music Harmony Workbook**
- **AS Music Composition Workbook**
- **AS Music Literacy Workbook**
- **Writing About Music Workbook**
- **Understanding Popular Music**
- **Careers in Music**
- **Music Technology from Scratch**
- **Dictionary of Music in Sound**

Contents

Introduction 5

AoS1 Western Classical tradition 1650–1910 7

AoS2 Pop music 47

AoS3 Music for media 59

AoS4 Music for theatre 72

AoS5 Jazz 83

AoS6 Contemporary traditional music 93

Performance and composition 104

Answers 106

Glossary 126

The authors

Richard Bristow

studied Music at Jesus College, Oxford, before completing his PGCE at the University of Southampton. Richard is currently Director of Music in a highly-successful independent school in London where he oversees the music curriculum and the extensive co-curricular programme.

He also has significant experience as a senior examiner at A Level, specialising in composition, as well as working for Keynote Education to deliver student conferences and teacher courses across the UK. Richard is active as both a performer and a composer; the BBC Singers have recorded his setting of the 'Agnus Dei' and he can regularly be found singing with various choirs in London and the South.

Richard Knight

read Music at St John's College, Oxford, and has been Director of Music at two leading independent schools. He also has nearly 20 years' experience as a senior examiner at A level and is also an examiner for the ABRSM in the UK and overseas.

Richard is a prolific composer with a large catalogue to his name including opera, orchestral, chamber and instrumental works (see www.rokmusic.org.uk). His works have been performed at the Tête à Tête Opera Festival in London and in various recitals in the UK and elsewhere. Some of his Christmas church music has been performed by the Ex Cathedra and Tenebrae choirs, and his *Preludes for Piano* are being recorded by the pianist Naomi Kayayan in 2017. Richard also conducts the Malvern Festival Chorus. He has a particular interest in all things South American.

Introduction

The fact that you have picked up this Revision Guide must mean your AS examination is getting close.

Here you will find some useful reminders:

- How the paper structured
- How many marks each section is worth
- Which Area of Study is relevant to each section

All being well you will feel confident that you have covered all the topics and set works required. There is plenty more information and detail about these in the Rhinegold Education *AQA AS and A Level Study Guide*.

In the exam room what is being tested is your understanding of music. The test is partly aural – the music you are given to listen to – and partly knowledge-based – the vocabulary and technical explanations of what the musical terms mean.

Of course, in the exam you are on your own; working through this book by yourself in advance is a good way to check how confident you are about the knowledge required. There are exercises to check yourself, and prompts to start and organise your revision process.

In the end no author or teacher can put the knowledge into your head unaided – that is down to you. Give the revision process your full focus, uninterrupted by distractions, and be determined to keep at it until you know that you know it, and your understanding is complete.

About Unit 1: Appraising Music

Unit 1: Appraising Music is the written examination of the AQA AS Music qualification.

The examination lasts for 2 hours and is divided into three sections relating to different musical skills and Areas of Study (AoS):

Section A: Listening

- Answer *all* questions on AoS1: Western Classical tradition 1650-1910

  Two strands of study:

  - The Baroque solo concerto
  - The operas of Mozart
- Answer *all* questions on **one** other AoS (2-6 from the list below)

Section B: Analysis

- Answer **one** question from a choice of two relating to the two strands in AoS1

Section C: Essay

Answer **one** essay from **one** AoS from 2-6. There is only one question for each AoS.

Using this revision guide

This book is divided into different chapters, each relating to a different AoS. For the AS Level examination, you must study AoS1 and **one** other AoS from the following:

- AoS2: Pop music
- AoS3: Music for media
- AoS4: Music for theatre
- AoS5: Jazz
- AoS6: Contemporary traditional music

AoS1 requires you to learn lots of specific musical vocabulary, much of which also features in AoS2-6. It is important that you work through this first chapter, developing your understanding of the different strands and completing the exercises to aid your knowledge.

The chapters that follow are set up to aid your general musicality, develop your listening skills, and revise the specific musical concepts inherent in each of the AoS. While you could only look at the single chapter relating to your chosen AoS, it would be more beneficial to work through each of the chapters, allowing your vocabulary and musical understanding to expand. The listening questions in each chapter might use the named artists for that specific AoS but are often based on similar concepts, allowing you to develop your listening skills and gain all-important examination practice. Relish the chance to expand your musical horizons!

There is a glossary beginning on page 126 which contains many of the musical terms you will need to know for this exam.

Western Classical tradition 1650–1910

Introduction

AoS1 is different to the remaining AoS in a number of important ways:

- It is compulsory
- The musical elements vocabulary for this AoS can also be tested in questions relating to other AoS
- Listening questions will involve an aural dictation question (Q.3)
- It involves the study of specified set works
- You have to answer **one** Section B question based on the set works
- You do <u>not</u> write an essay on AoS1 music

> The AQA AS Music specification can be found at www.aqa.org.uk/ subjects/music/as-and-a-level/music-7271. This contains a full list of the relevant vocabulary for each AoS. Further examples and explanations can be found in the *AQA AS and A Level Music Study Guide* (Rhinegold Education).

Strands and set works

There are two strands to this AoS at AS level:

- Baroque: the solo concerto
- Classical: the operas of Mozart

In Section A, the listening questions will be based on music that belongs to these strands, but will **not** use music from your set works.

The listening questions will be structured as follows:

Q1	An extract from a Baroque solo concerto	4 marks
Q2	An extract from an opera by Mozart	4 marks
Q3	An extract from either a solo concerto or a Mozart opera used as the basis for an aural dictation question	6 marks
Q4	Here you will have the choice to explain **either** which features of the music in Question 1 are typical of Baroque music, **or** which features of the music in Question 2 are typical of the Classical period	10 marks

The set works you will have studied for AS are:

Baroque solo concerto:

- Purcell: Sonata for trumpet and strings in D major Z.850 – all three movements

- Vivaldi: Flute Concerto in D major Op. 10 No. 3 'Il Gardellino' RV 428 – first movement only

- Bach: Violin Concerto in A minor BWV1041 – first movement only

The operas of Mozart:

- The Marriage of Figaro (*Le Nozze di Figaro*) K.492, Act I

  The following numbers only:

  - No. 1 Duettino (Figaro and Susanna, including following recitative)

  - No. 3 Cavatina (Figaro, including the previous recitative)

  - No. 4 Aria (Bartolo)

  - No. 5 Duettino (Susanna and Marcellina)

  - No. 6 Aria (Cherubino)

Musical language for this Area of Study

An important part of your revision in this Area of Study should be the technical vocabulary listed in the specification.

All the terms found here can also be tested in your optional Areas of Study, so they should be a priority for your revision.

The following exercises should enable you to check your understanding of these important words by looking at short musical examples. In Section A of the Appraising Music paper you have to be able to do this in response to the *sound* and not the score, so it is recommended that while doing these exercises by looking at the music given, you also play the tunes and listen to how they sound while thinking of the relevant vocabulary.

Meanwhile, this method of revising the terms – by seeing examples of each term in notation – should directly help you to prepare for the analysis questions in Section B of the Appraising Music paper.

Melody words

Exercise 1 – Contours

Study the following melody and fill in the bar numbers that match the descriptions of the melodic **contour** in the chart underneath:

Description	Bar number(s)
An ascending scalic contour	
A descending scalic contour	
An ascending arpeggio contour	

| A descending arpeggio contour |
| A triadic contour |
| A conjunct (non-scalic) contour |
| A disjunct contour |

Exercise 2 – Special melodic notes

Consider the following piece and describe the function of the notes specified in the chart below it by using the appropriate words from the following list:

- **Passing notes** – accented, unaccented, chromatic
- **Auxiliary notes** – upper, lower, chromatic
- **Appoggiatura**
- **Note of anticipation**
- **Echappée note**

Position (bar/beat)	Note name	Description
1²	C	
1³	A	
4¹	A	
4²	F	
5¹	C♯	
6¹	A	
7¹	F♯	
11³	D	
12¹	A	
12³	B♭	

Exercise 3 – Intervals

Using the previous piece (see Exercise 2) identify the following intervals in the melodic line:

Bar	Notes	Interval
2	D – G	
3	D – B♭	
3-4	F – A	
11	E♭ – C	
11	F – E♭	
13	E♭ – A	

Exercise 4 – Melodic devices

The vocabulary for this exercise includes:

- **Motif**
- **Sequence** – rising and falling
- **Fragmentation**
- **Inversion**
- **Intervallic augmentation** and **diminution**

Study the melody of the piece below and then answer the questions that follow.

Questions about the melodic line (tick each correct answer):

1. **Bars 1-10 comprise:**

    six phrases of imbalanced lengths ☐

    two balanced 5-bar phrases ☐

    one long phrase of 10 bars ☐

2. **The first four notes are best described as:**

    Theme ☐

    Phrase ☐

    Motif ☐

3. **The A♯ in bar 2 is...**

    A chromatic passing note ☐

    A lower chromatic auxiliary note ☐

    A chromatic appoggiatura ☐

4. **Compare bars 6²-7¹ with bars 1²-2¹. The technique used is:**

    Repetition ☐

    Sequence ☐

    Intervallic augmentation ☐

5. **Compare bars 14-16 with bars 11-13. The technique used is:**

    Repetition ☐

    Rising sequence ☐

    Falling sequence ☐

6. **Compare bars 17²-18¹ with bars 1²-2¹. The technique used is:**

    Fragmentation and inversion ☐

    Fragmentation and sequence ☐

    Intervallic diminution and inversion ☐

7. **In bars 19-20 the technique used is:**

Fragmentation ☐

Repetition ☐

Rising sequence ☐

8. **The melodic contour in bar 24 is best described as:**

Disjunct ☐

Triadic ☐

Arpeggio ☐

9. **The sequence in bars 25-28 is:**

Falling by step ☐

Falling by a 3rd ☐

Falling by a 4th ☐

10. **In bars 30-33 the technique used is:**

Sequence ☐

Fragmentation ☐

Repetition ☐

Exercise 5 – Ornamentation

Complete the table below by naming each of the ornaments given and assigning them the correct notation for how they are played, choosing from A-F in the following examples.

Ornament symbol	Ornament name	How played: give letter name to show which example above is the written-out form of this ornament
A		
B		
C		
D		
E		
F		

Harmony words

Exercise 6 – Diatonic chords and inversions

The **diatonic** chords are usually labelled using Roman numerals (I-VII) with 'b' added for 1st inversions and 'c' for 2nd inversions. V^{7}d is the 3rd inversion of the dominant 7th (with the 7th in the bass). It is often the custom to use capital Roman numerals for chords which are major, and lower case for chords which are minor (with italics sometimes used for diminished chords).

Here are the chords of C major and A minor:

Identify the chords of the following piece in B♭ major by putting Roman numerals underneath each one.

Exercise 7 – Cadences

You need to be familiar with the following cadences:

Perfect	V to I	including the common approach via Ic (a **cadential 6/4**)
Plagal	IV to I	also known as the 'Amen cadence'
Interrupted	V to a surprise	often vi (other options include I♭⁷b or a diminished 7th)
Imperfect	various to V	including Ic to V (known as a **half-close**), and ivb to V (known as a **Phrygian** cadence)

Now consider the music below and fill in the chart for each of the cadences in the piece.

Bar	Key	Chords	Cadence
2			
4			
6			
8			
10			
12			
14			
16			
18			
20	G major	V – I	Perfect (NB 4-3 suspension on V)

Exercise 8 – Advanced chords

In addition to diatonic chords, you need to be familiar with handling and analysing the following more advanced harmonic options:

- Diminished 7ths
- Secondary dominant 7ths
- **Substitution chords** (e.g. iv in a major key)
- **Chord of the Neapolitan**
- Augmented 6th chords (Italian, German and French)
- **Tierce de Picardie**

Study the following music and then analyse the chords listed in the chart underneath:

Chord	Chord analysis
Bar 3^2	
Bar 5^1	
Bar 5^2	
Bar 7^2	
Bar 9^2	
Bar 11	

AoS1 MUSICAL LANGUAGE

Bar 13[2]	
Bar 18	
Bar 19[1]	
Bar 22	

Exercise 9 – Keys: signatures and relationships

By this stage your understanding of the tonal system should be strong.
Test yourself with this quiz:

1. How many sharps are in B major?

2. How many flats are in A♭ flat major?

3. What is the relative minor of E♭ major?

4. What is the relative major of F♯ minor?

5. When a piece in F minor modulates to its dominant, to which key does it change?

6. Which major key has 4 sharps?

7. Which minor key has 5 flats?

8. When a piece in B minor modulates to its subdominant, to which key does it change?

9. What key is the enharmonic equivalent of D♯ minor?

10. If a piece in B major modulates to the enharmonic equivalent of its median major, to which key does it change?

Texture words

It can be tempting to think that the answer to every texture question is a single word ending in -*phony*. This is not a helpful instinct to have.

There are three aspects to texture:

- How many notes are used at any given point?
- In what context or role do each of these notes belong?
- In which registers do the notes occur?

The possible contexts or roles include: melody, doubling of melody at a 3rd (or other interval), countermelody, imitative contrapuntal line, bass line, pedal note, accompaniment figuration, inner part to chord, and so on.

Only when you have considered these angles should you reach for a texture label word; sometimes it is best to describe a texture without using a -*phony* word.

Test yourself on the definition of these terms by filling in the table:

Texture term	Definition
Monophonic	
Unison	
Octaves texture	
Parallel 3rds	
Melody and accompaniment	
Homophonic	
Polyphonic	
Contrapuntal	
Fugal	
Canonic	
Antiphonal	

Tempo, metre and rhythm words

What you need to know:

- Italian terms for tempo: (from slow to fast) grave, adagio, lento, largo, larghetto, andante, moderato, allegretto, allegro, vivace, presto, prestissimo
- Terms that cause tempo to change: ritenuto, rallentando, rubato, accelerando
- The difference between **simple time** (the beat subdivides into two, such as $\frac{2}{4}$, $\frac{3}{4}$, $\frac{4}{4}$) and **compound time** (the beat subdivides into three, such as $\frac{6}{8}$ and others, giving two main beats in a bar)

Dynamics and articulation words

What you need to know:

- The normal Italian abbreviations for dynamics from **_pp_** to **_ff_**, and also **_sfz_** and **_fp_**
- The signs and sounds of different standard types of articulation: accent, **legato**, **marcato**, **staccato**, and **tenuto** (see the glossary at the back of the book)

Sonority and timbre words

What you need to know:

- The names and sounds of all standard orchestral instruments and vocal types. You may need to hear the difference between a viola and a cello, an oboe and a bassoon, or a soprano and a mezzo-soprano
- The name and sound of special techniques that are applicable to these instruments. For example:
  - Strings: **pizzicato**, **arco**, **sul tasto**, **sul ponticello**, **col legno**, **con sordino**, **double stopping**
  - Singing: **Sotto voce**, **portamento** and **vibrato**

Structure words

What you need to know:

You need to understand what is meant by the following terms:

- **Binary form**
- **Rounded binary form**
- **Ternary form**
- **Ritornello** and **episode**
- **Recitative**
- **Aria**
- **Sonata form**
- **Through-composed**

See the glossary at the back of the book for any terms you are unsure about.

Remember: you are now a specialist music student and should be using this vocabulary like it is your mother tongue!

Practice for Section A questions on AoS1

Preparing for question 1

Question 1 will be a short extract of Baroque concerto worth 4 marks. The questions could be about any element of music (melody, rhythm, harmony, texture, structure, and so on). Due to the style and genre of music being set, likely questions include:

- Identifying the solo instrument
- Understanding whether the passage is a **ritornello** or solo passage
- Commenting on the **basso continuo** (if present)
- Spotting harmonic progressions such as rising sequences of **circle of 5ths** patterns
- Identifying modulations

Of course, the best way to prepare for this question is to listen (actively, with your mind focused on the music) frequently to a wide range of different concertos from the period. Good composers to explore include Corelli, Vivaldi, Handel, Torelli, Locatelli, and Bach. Try listening to concertos for as many different solo instruments as you can find (such as violin, viola d'amore, cello, flute, oboe, bassoon, trumpet, harpsichord, organ, and mandolin).

Here is a much more substantial question for you to work through which covers many of these different areas.

QUESTION 1

This question uses Vivaldi's Concerto RV495, first movement, which can be found at: http://bit.ly/VivaldiRV495

Extract for this exam paper: 0:45-2:45

You will hear the start of a solo concerto by Vivaldi. The music is in $\frac{3}{8}$ time, and the home key is G minor.

1. The movement begins with a tutti section. What is the opening interval in the melodic line? Underline your answer.

    Perfect 4th   Perfect 5th   Octave   Perfect 12th

2. What is the texture of the string instruments in the opening section?

3. What is the tonality of the music in the opening section?

AoS1 SECTION A

4. Which of the following is heard in the opening tutti section?

   Circle of 5ths harmony   **Neapolitan 6th**

   Rising sequence   **Tonic pedal**

5. What is the solo instrument?

6. There are three main subsections to the first solo passage.
   Which of the following is an accurate description? (Tick your answer):

   a. A passage over a descending bass played twice
      A passage based on a rising harmonic sequence
      A passage over a descending bass with slower
      harmonic rhythm

   b. A passage over a descending bass played twice
      A passage based on circle of 5ths harmony
      A passage over a descending bass with faster
      harmonic rhythm

   c. A passage over a descending bass played twice
      A passage based on circle of 5ths harmony
      A passage over a descending bass with slower
      harmonic rhythm

   d. A passage over a descending bass played twice
      A passage based on a rising harmonic sequence
      A passage over a descending bass with faster
      harmonic rhythm

7. In which key does the second ritornello start?

8. To which key does the second ritornello change after two short
   phrases, and then finish?

9. Early in the second solo section there is a rising sequence.
   How many bars long is the phrase that is used for this sequence?
   Underline your answer.

   1 bar   **2 bars**   **3 bars**   **4 bars**

10. Name the harmonic device that Vivaldi uses for the central
    portion of the second solo section.

11. In what key is a shortened ritornello heard after the second solo section? Underline your answer.

Relative major   **Relative of the subdominant**

Relative of the dominant   **Tonic major**

12. The final solo passage heard also starts with a sequence. Which of the following is an accurate description of this solo? Tick your answer.

a. A rising shape treated to rising sequence ☐

b. A passage over a descending bass played twice ☐

c. A falling shape treated to rising sequence ☐

d. A falling shape treated to falling sequence ☐

Preparing for Question 2

Question 2 will be a short extract from a Mozart opera worth 4 marks. The questions could be about any element of music (melody, rhythm, harmony, texture, structure, and so on). Due to the style and genre of music being set, likely questions include:

- Identifying the voice type (soprano, bass, and so on)
- Spotting what type of movement is being heard (recitative, aria, and so on)
- Commenting on the vocal line (range, intervals, ornaments, and so on)
- Hearing how the singer is accompanied – texture and instrumentation
- Analysing cadences

Of course, the best way to prepare for this question is to listen frequently (and actively, with your mind focused on the music) to items from Mozart's many operas. Best of all, try to get to a performance of one of them – a night out at the theatre! In addition to the opera that provides your set work movements – *The Marriage of Figaro* – other famous operas by Mozart include *Idomeneo*, *Così fan tutte* and *The Magic Flute*.

QUESTION 2

Here is a much more substantial question for you to work through which covers many of these different areas.

The question uses an aria from *The Magic Flute* called 'O Isis und Osiris' sung by Sarastro, the High Priest of the Sun. The German words and a translation are as follows:

SARASTRO:

1.	O Isis und Osiris, schenket	O Isis and Osiris, give
2.	Der Weisheit Geist dem neuen Paar!	The spirit of wisdom to the new pair.
3.	Die ihr der Wand'rer Schritte lenket,	She who links to her the wanderer's steps,
4.	Stärkt mit Geduld sie in Gefahr,	Strengthens them with patience in danger,
5.	Stärkt mit Geduld sie in Gefahr.	Strengthens them with patience in danger.

CHORUS:

6.	Stärkt mit Geduld sie in Gefahr.	Strengthens them with patience in danger.

SARASTRO:

7.	Lasst sie der Prüfung Früchte sehen;	Let them see the fruits of the test;
8.	Doch sollten sie zu Grabe gehen,	But, if they should go to the grave,
9.	So lohnt der Tugend kühnen Lauf,	Then, the valiant course of virtue rewarded,
10.	Nehmt sie in euren Wohnsitz auf,	Receive them in your abode,
11.	Nehmt sie in euren Wohnsitz auf,	Receive them in your abode.

CHORUS:

12.	Nehmt sie in euren Wohnsitz auf,	Receive them in your abode.

The music can be found at: http://bit.ly/MozartIsisOsiris

1. What voice type is the singer? Underline your answer.

Countertenor   Tenor   Baritone   Bass

2. What is the metre of the music?

3. What is the most appropriate tempo marking for the music? Underline your answer.

   Adagio   Andante   Allegretto   Moderato

4. On which degree of the scale does the vocal line begin? Underline your answer.

   Tonic   Mediant   Dominant   Leading note

5. Which word best describes of the vocal contour for line 2? Underline your answer.

   Arpeggio   Disjunct   Scalic   Triadic

6. Identify the interval of the rising leap on 'Schritte' in line 3. Underline your answer.

   Major 6th   Minor 7th   Major 7th   Octave

7. What cadence occurs on 'in Gefahr' at the end of line 5? Underline your answer.

   Ic – V^7 – I   Ic – V^7 – VI   ii7b – V^7 – I   ii7b – V^7 – VI

8. Identify the choral texture in line 6. Underline your answer.

   Antiphonal   Octaves   Homophony   Polyphony

9. What chord underpins 'Prüfung Früchte' in line 7? Underline your answer.

   Augmented 6th   Diminished 7th

   Neapolitan 6th   Secondary 7th

10. In which two lines of text does the singer have the same line as the bass of the orchestra?

11. Which combination of wind instruments is playing in the orchestra? Tick your answer.

    a. Oboes, Clarinets and Horns ☐

    b. Oboes, Bassoons and Horns ☐

    c. Clarinets, Bassoons and Trombones ☐

    d. Trumpets, Clarinets and Bassoons ☐

12. Which of the following is the correct description of the key scheme of this aria? Tick your answer.

    a. The music modulates to the dominant halfway through and stays there to the end ☐

    b. The music modulates to the relative minor and returns to the tonic in the second half ☐

    c. The music modulates to the relative minor and then ends in the dominant ☐

    d. The music modulates to the dominant halfway ☐

Preparing for question 3

Question 3 tests your ability to notate the music you hear, a skill called 'aural dictation'. This is a very useful ability to have; like so many musical talents, it takes practice – you can't really 'revise' it the week before an exam. You should try to do some every day. You can try writing down ringtones, sirens, theme tunes, tunes you are learning to play (without looking at the music!), and so on.

QUESTION 3

Here are two useful challenges:

1. Write down the tune for the British national anthem. The first two bars have been given for you:

2. Write down the tune for 'Happy Birthday'. The first two bars have been given for you:

Preparing for question 4

Question 4 will be the same wording each year (but about a different piece of music!). It goes as follows:

QUESTION 4

Choose the music from question 1 or question 2. Explain which features of the music help you to identify that it is from the Baroque period (question 1) or the Classical period (question 2).

There are 10 marks available on this question.

It is very important that you answer this question referring in detail to the piece of music you have chosen to write about. The examiners are **not** asking 'What are the typical features of a Baroque concerto/Mozart's operas?' You need to listen carefully to identify specific aspects of the music they have set for your exam paper.

You are advised to spend 25 minutes on questions 1-4, and 10 of the 24 marks are for question 4, so you should take time to consider all the different angles: melody, rhythm, harmony and tonality, texture, instrumentation and structure.

Among the aspects you might listen out for are:

Baroque concerto	Mozart opera
Melody	**Melody**
A **ritornello** with a strong head motif	**Antecedent** and **consequent phrases**
Solo passagework based on **triadic** patterns	**Periodic phrasing**
Trills and **mordents**	Scalic and triadic contours
Harmony	**Trills** and **turns**
Rising sequences	**Appoggiaturas** and accented passing notes
Circle of 5ths progression (with 7ths maybe)	**Harmony**
Use of **suspensions**	Heavy reliance on I and V
Texture	Significant structural cadences using **cadential 6/4**
Unison strings in the **ripieno**	**Texture**
Polarised texture of soloist and bass line	Simple bass line
Active bass line	Use of delicate accompaniment figures
Rhythm	**Rhythm**
Long runs of semiquavers	Answering phrases having the same rhythm
Anacrusis	Possible use of triplets
Dotted patterns	
Instrumentation	**Instrumentation**
Use of **basso continuo**	Presence of a woodwind section in the orchestra – maybe including clarinets
Harpsichord and/or lute	Horns used to blend orchestra together
Structure	**Structure**
Contrast between tutti and solo passages	Possible use of **Recitative**
Fragmentation of the **ritornello** to provide accompanying **motifs**	Significant use of modulation to V

Practice for Section B questions

Section B is based upon your study of the set works. There are **two** questions, and you have to answer only **one** of them:

- Question 25: Baroque solo concerto
- Question 26: Mozart opera

In each case a single, substantial passage of music will be the basis of the question. This will be provided both as an audio track and in score form on the question paper.

There are 17 marks available; 7 of these are for short answer questions identifying specific analytical details, and the other 10 are for a long answer addressing the whole extract from a specific analytical angle (such as melodic writing, harmonic content, use of instruments and so on).

It is recommended that you spend 25 minutes answering your chosen question.

SAMPLE QUESTION 25

Use your favourite recording of Vivaldi's Concerto 'Il Gardellino' in conjunction with this score and the question beneath.

a piacimento

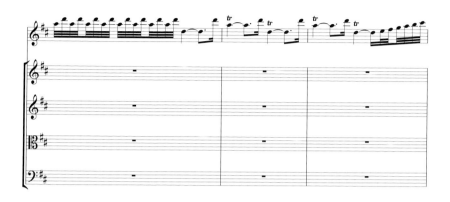

1. What is the interval between the last note of bar 5 and the first note of bar 6 in the 1st violin?   [1 mark]

2. What is the name of the harmonic progression used in bars 5-8?   [1 mark]

3. Which two keys are visited in bars 34^3-39^2?   [2 marks]

4. What chord is implied by the figures $^6_5$ under the bass E in bar 36?   [2 marks]

5. Give a bar and beat number where the viola bass line is a compound diminished 7th below the 1st violins in the passage between bars 37-47.   [1 mark]

6. Discuss the composer's handling of melody, tonality and texture in the extract, showing how he creates structure from these elements. In your answer you should make reference to specific details in the score.   [10 marks]

[Total: 17 marks]

SAMPLE QUESTION 26

Use your favourite recording of the opening duettino from *The Marriage of Figaro,* in conjunction with this score and the question beneath.

1. Explain how the tied C in the bass of the accompaniment in bars 8-9 changes function by considering the following moments:

   bar 8³ _____

   bar 9¹ _____   [2 marks]

2. What term best describes Susanna's melodic contour in bars 17³-18³?   [1 mark]

3. What falling interval does Figaro sing in bar 28?   [1 mark]

4. What harmonic device does Mozart use in bars 29-32²?   [2 marks]

5. What term describes the vocal texture in bars 38-42?   [1 mark]

6. Comment on melody, harmony and tonality, and rhythm, and show how Mozart uses the conventions of a sonata form exposition in this passage of music to portray his two characters.

   In your answer you should make reference to specific details in the score.   [10 marks]

   [Total: 17 marks]

Revising the set works

General advice

The movements that AQA have set as set works will contain the passages that are set in Section B of your written paper. Therefore, the better you know these pieces,

- the more fluently you will be able to work in the 25 minutes you spend answering the question you have chosen
- the more you will be able to write accurate analytical detail (rather than general overview commentary)
- the more marks you will get!

So how do you get to know these set movements? There are a number of ways; some will seem obvious, others perhaps less so:

- Listening to recorded performances of the music
- Listening to recorded performances while following the score
- Reading the score silently, without listening to the music (like reading a novel)
- Playing/singing the music – maybe you play the instrument(s) intended by the composers, maybe your school orchestra can tackle one of the pieces, however....
- ...one of the best ways is to make your own arrangement of the music for you and your friends to play: maybe in a wind quintet, a brass group, a 'Swingle Singers' style vocal group, or a rock band

Ultimately, if you want the best understanding you can gain, you need to approach the pieces in as many guises as you can: listener, analyst, performer, arranger, and so on. This way your brain will make connections between all these experiences; these connections will be *your* understanding of the music.

There is a lot of analytical detail in the *AS and A level Music Study Guide* (Rhinegold Education). Over the next few pages is a series of prompts for each of the set pieces – angles which you ought to think about when you are revising these pieces.

Remember: ultimately the examiners are looking for evidence of your understanding of the music; this is far more important than trying to memorise lots of information that someone else has written and which is only based on *their* understanding.

Baroque solo concerto

Purcell: Sonata for trumpet and strings in D major Z.850
General points to consider:

- The significance of the harmonic series to the 17th century trumpet
- The lack of valves limiting the notes available to the trumpeter
- Purcell's interest in unusual harmonic twists
- The piece pre-dates the popularity of **ritornello** form

First movement:

- Melodic contours that use quaver rests, pairs of semiquavers, leaps of 4ths and 5ths, trills
- Textures that include simple detached chords, a partial **fugal** dimension, **antiphony** between trumpet and strings, string activity under an **inverted pedal** on the trumpet
- Unusual passages of harmonic writing
- Contrast between sections created by subtle changes of rhythm/note value

Second movement:

- How contrast is created with the previous movement through instrumentation, tonality and texture
- Purcell's interest in chromatic harmony and the open 5th at bar 4^3

Third movement:

- The gigue-like character generated by the rhythmic profile
- The use of **hemiola** at cadences (for example in bars 80-81)
- The extent to which the texture is **contrapuntal/fugal**
- The skilful blend of **conjunct** melodic contour and large leaps, and the use of **melodic inversion** at bar 82

Vivaldi: Flute concerto in D major Op. 10 No. 3 'Il Gardellino' RV428
First movement:

- **Ritornello** form: the main sections (tutti/solo) and key centres
- The melodic contour of the ritornello theme and its constituent ideas
- Use of circle of 5ths harmonic patterns and rising sequences
- The virtuosity of the flute part, its bird-like aspects, its interplay with the violins in the **ripieno**

- The variety of the bass line throughout the movement, including the octaves texture of the ritornello, long pedal notes in the cello, and passages where the violas provide a 'walking' bass line
- The role of the **basso continuo**

Bach: Violin Concerto in A minor BWV1041

First movement:

- Ritornello form: the main sections and key centres
- The importance of the initial anacrusis with its rising 4th which pervades so much of the music
- The intricacies of the melodic line with its rhythmic drive (**anacruses**, tied notes, flowing semiquavers) and harmonically focused contour (including **sequences**)
- The active bass line with scales, **auxiliary notes** and moments of strong angularity (for example leaps of a diminished 7th)
- Complexities of harmonic progressions – not just **circle of 5ths** but the use of **Neapolitan chords** from bar 135
- Changes of harmonic rhythm

Mozart opera: *The Marriage of Figaro*, Act 1 (selected numbers)

General points:

- The use of twinned phrases, tonic-dominant harmony and articulating cadences
- The influence of sonata form as an element of the style of the music – especially modulating to the dominant for a secondary theme/idea
- Melodies that use scalic and triadic shapes
- Mozart's skill at using the musical vernacular of his day to portray a range of human personalities and motivations

No. 1 Duettino:

- The use of **sonata form** principles with the first subject representing Figaro and the second subject representing Susanna. He ends up singing her tune!
- Parallel contrasts of melodic contour, **syllabic**/non-syllabic word-setting, and instrumentation in the accompaniment
- The variety of textures between the two vocal parts
- Reasons why the recapitulation is shorter than the exposition

No. 3 Cavatina:

- The unusual ABCA structure
- The influence of the Menuet on the music: 4-bar phrases, **diatonic** harmony, simple rhythms
- The use and significance of the horns
- The more elaborate texture and harmonic palette of the B section in response to the text
- The additional dimension of characterisation in the C section

No. 4 Aria:

- The use of **sonata exposition** in bars 1-50
- The portrayal of Bartolo's assertive character through a **disjunct** melody of wide register
- Aspects of the music that convey rage including: running semiquavers, staccato wind chords, harmonic adventure including an augmented 6th chord in bar 46-48
- A free-flowing middle section with a long line of triplet quavers to test the singer

No. 5 Duettino:

- The juxtaposition of elegant melody and restless triplets in the orchestra
- The relationship of the two singers' vocal lines

No. 6 Aria:

- The **ternary** form of the opening section (bars 1-51)
- The ways in which the first section conveys impetuousness through rhythm, intervallic augmentation, quickening harmonic rhythm and placement of the top note in the melodic contour
- Use of chromaticism and **appoggiaturas** to suggest sighing
- The instrumentation including the clarinets
- Mozart's skill in the second half of the aria in creating a thrilling ending to a 'show-stopper' number

Pop music

Introduction

This is an exciting, contemporary and probably familiar Area of Study looking at pop music and the development of the genre.

There are six named artists in this AoS for you to listen to, study, and gain a critical appreciation of. You should seek to establish *how* they create their particular sound world by detailed analytical study of their music.

For the purpose of this specification, pop music is defined as popular mainstream music derived from and including a number of musical genres, including rock, funk and R&B, from 1960 to the present.

- Stevie Wonder
- Joni Mitchell
- Muse
- Beyoncé
- Daft Punk
- Labrinth

This chapter will look at accessing the key vocabulary listed in the AQA specification, with some sample listening questions similar to Section A and a sample essay for Section C of the written paper.

> The AQA AS Music specification can be found at www.aqa.org.uk/subjects/music/as-and-a-level/music-7271. This contains a full list of the relevant vocabulary for each AoS. Further examples and explanations can be found in the *AQA AS and A Level Music Study Guide* (Rhinegold Education).

Musical language for this Area of Study

In addition to a full working knowledge of the vocabulary listed for AoS1, AoS2 also requires you to be familiar with specific vocabulary found in the music of the named artists.

The following approach can be used for the pieces you have studied to ensure you are familiar with these musical concepts. The answers can be found at the back of the book.

Harmonic analysis

Chord symbols are an essential part of this AoS and having a good working knowledge of chord symbols, advanced chords and chromatic chords will greatly help your understanding. Complete the following exercise, writing out the chord in staff notation.

A good way of approaching this is to:

1. Establish the major or minor triad

2. Observe whether the bass is in **root** or **inversion**

3. Establish whether the chord is extended – for example 7th, 9th, 11th, 13th – or diminished (º) or augmented (⁺)

4. Establish if there is a **suspension** (for example sus4), **pedal point**, or additional added notes

D⁷/F♯   G   C⁷   C♯dim   Dsus4

Use of studio/technological effects

Many pieces in this AoS are processed using advanced music technology software. It is vital that you understand and can hear these processes.

- **Chorus**: two individual sounds with similar timbral qualities and pitch placed together to sound as one. 'Timbral' relates to the timbre of a sound, which is its particular quality or tone colour

- **Delay**: a controlled echo which is repeated at a specified time, often getting quieter with each repetition

- **Reverb**: electronically-produced echo
- **Distortion**: often used on electric guitars by increasing the gain, giving a different timbre
- **Panning**: using the left and right parts of the stereo field

STUDY PIECE 1

Stevie Wonder, 'Sir Duke'

You can find this song here: http://bit.ly/StevieWonderSirDuke

The opening bars of this piece are iconic and contain many of the melodic and harmonic features listed in the specification. Listen to the introduction, observing the following table, which has been partially completed for you. Read the description below which explains the crosses in the table.

Stevie Wonder – 'Sir Duke'

		Intro	Verse	Chorus
Tonality	Blues Scale	X		
	Pentatonic			
	Mode use			
Harmony	Pedal Point	X		
	Chord Symbols	X		
	Complex chords			
	Chord Extensions			
	Sus4 chords			
	Power Chords			

Melody	Blue Notes	X
	Glissando/Slide	X
	Hook	X
	Syllabic	
	Melisma	
	Pitch Bend	X
	Riff/Ostinato	X

Having listened to the introduction you may have noticed the following:

The opening one bar **riff/ostinato** using an ascending **broken chord** which is embellished rhythmically on each repetition. This acts as a memorable one bar **hook**.

- The use of brass slide/**glissando** between D-G in the third repetition
- Use of ♯4th/♭5th in the hook, using the **blues scale/notes**
- The N.C. bar chord symbol and the bass dominant pedal before the verse starts the groove

The *AQA AS and A Level Music Study Guide* (Rhinegold Education) contains useful pointers on how to analyse this piece.

Completing your aural analysis

Now complete the table for the verse and chorus which follow, adding a cross for each feature you hear in the music. Having done this, write a short bullet point to give greater musical analysis to your point, as in the example above. You may wish to add this to your own musical glossary for the elements, listing where you can hear them.

By creating your own musical glossary, similar to the one at the back of this revision guide, you will be able to cross reference quickly where musical devices occur, allowing for more effective revision.

STUDY PIECE 2

Beyoncé, 'Best Thing I Never Had'

You can find this song here: http://bit.ly/BTINHbeyonce

If you have worked through the *AQA AS and A Level Music Study Guide*, you should already have completed an independent analysis for this song, to work alongside the analysis of other works by Beyoncé presented in that book.

Listen to the song and write down the lyrics where the following timbral aspects are employed:

1. Vocal belt

2. Backing vocals in 3rds

3. Vocal embellishment

The piece uses a **backbeat** throughout, accenting the 4th quaver beat which is then tied to a minim. Notice how the texture changes at 'I know you want me back', reducing significantly with a higher **tessitura** and increased vocal decoration.

Listening (Section A)

There will be four pieces to listen to and answer questions on in this part of the paper. Here is a sample Section A of the exam paper covering AoS2.

Track 1 – Muse, 'Plug in Baby'

Listen to this song, which you can find here: http://bit.ly/MusePlugInBaby

Extract: 0:00-1:03 (to end of first verse)

1. Which instrument plays the opening riff?   [1 mark]

2. What is the harmonic rhythm of the introduction?
   Underline your answer:

   1 chord every bar   **2 chords every bar**

   2 chords every 2 bars   **1 chord every 2 bars**   [1 mark]

3. What is the range of the vocal line in the first two lines
   of the verse?   [2 marks]

4. What is an appropriate tempo marking for this song?
   Underline your answer:

   90bpm   **115bpm**   **135bpm**   **150bpm**   [1 mark]

   [Total: 5 marks]

Question 3 is worth 2 marks so the answer requires two parts.

Track 2 – Joni Mitchell, 'Both Sides Now' (2000 orchestral version)

Listen to this song, which you can find here: http://bit.ly/JoniMitchellBSN

Extract: 1:10-1:46 (first chorus)

1. What is the time signature of this extract?   [1 mark]

2. On which degree of the scale does the vocal melody start?   [1 mark]

3. Which **one** of the rhythm patterns below is used in the drum kit?

a. ☐

b. ☐

c. ☐

d. ☐   [1 mark]

4. Which word best describes the harmony of the extract?

  Major   **Minor**   **Pentatonic**   **Modal**   [1 mark]

5. Which **one** of the following features can be heard in the instrumental accompaniment?

  Suspension   **Melisma**   **Mordent**   **Pitch bend**   [1 mark]

[Total: 5 marks]

Track 3 – Daft Punk, 'Get Lucky'

Listen to this song, which you can find here: http://bit.ly/DaftPunkGL

Extract: 0:00 – 1:20 (to end of first chorus)

1. The extract is based on a repeated four chord sequence.
   Tick the chord progression that shows the correct sequence.

   a. Bm   F♯   A   Bm   ☐

   b. Bm   F♯m   Gm   D   ☐

   c. Bm   D   F♯m   Bm   ☐

   d. Bm   D   F♯m   E   ☐   [1 mark]

2. On which **two** beats of the bar is the snare played?   [2 marks]

3. What is the range of the melody during the first line (4 bars)
   of the chorus 'We've come so far, to give up who we are'?
   Underline your answer.

   4th   5th   6th   7th   [1 mark]

4. Which **one** of these terms best describes the vocal line?
   Underline your answer.

   Conjunct   Chromatic   Disjunct   Triadic   [1 mark]

   [Total: 5 marks]

Question 1 can be worked out on a basic level by establishing the order of major and minor chords in the extract. This narrows down the possible correct answers.

[Total for Section A: 15 marks]

Essay question (Section C)

In the examination, you have to answer one essay question. There will be only one set for each AoS, so there is no choice beyond which AoS you have studied. You have 45 minutes to write the essay which is marked out of 30.

You can read the full mark scheme for this exam paper here: http://filestore.aqa.org.uk/resources/music/AQA-72711-SMS.PDF

This shows in detail the mark band breakdown for the essay question.

Remember to plan your essay fully before embarking on writing it. Then you will be sure not to forget any important points, but it will also help you to organise your time so that you don't run out.

Task – Essay Analysis

1. Read the sample essay below, look online at the mark scheme, and mark it yourself, considering:

   - The accuracy of musical vocabulary and detail
   - The use of supportive musical examples with detailed analysis
   - Whether the writing shows an aural awareness of the piece
   - The accuracy of spelling, grammar and written communication to give a mature writing style
   - Whether the essay answers the question fully

2. Compare your marks and thoughts with your peers to form a class discussion. How did your teacher mark the essay? Compare this to the marked copy in the answers section at the back of the book.

3. How can this candidate improve their mark? Write a teacher-style comment for the essay, including a target for improvement.

4. Now write the essay yourself, taking these ideas into consideration.

'A pop musician can encompass many genres of music during one career'

Selecting *two* pieces by *the same* named artist, consider how they demonstrate contrasting musical styles.

Piece 1: Stevie Wonder 'Superstition' (1972)

Piece 2: Stevie Wonder 'I just called to say I love you' (1984)

Funk as a genre of music emerged in 1960s America, itself a combination of musical styles. The key characteristics of funk include a complex groove, interjections from the horn section and interlocking drum patterns. 'Superstition' has many of these characteristics, with an opening riff which is now iconic. It uses the Eb minor pentatonic scale with four straight quavers followed by a more complex second part of the bar. The second clavinet part plays an Eb major 7 chord underneath this 2-bar riff, giving an Eb(b7#9) chord with the major and minor third played simultaneously. The bass guitar anchors the riff, playing on the beat Ebs before increased quaver movement in the final two beats of the bar. Wonder's vocals also employ the Ebm pentatonic scale with subtle syncopation over this accompaniment, dovetailing with the three-layered texture.

The piece develops in three main ways. Firstly, Wonder introduces a horn riff (tenor saxophone and trumpet) at 'thirteen month old baby'. This new riff has an ascending profile using semiquavers, again employing the pentatonic scale, peaking on a top Bb. The use of ties aids the syncopation. A second development occurs in the short chorus, where the harmonic rhythm changes to two chords per bar, outlining V7, bvi7 and V7 secondary dominant (V7b of V) in minims before settling on IV7 for a whole bar, eventually resolving to a crotchet V+ augmented triad on Bb. This chromatic chord allows for a one bar breakdown to interrupt the flow of the music. Finally, a 4-bar link with the horn section prominently using C natural in a contrasting descending pattern leads into the bridge which repeats the chorus chords complete with a vocal 'howl'.

In a similar way to how funk as a musical style developed from a combination of older musical styles, R&B also went through a similar transformation. Whilst the style could be argued to have started in 1940s America, by the 1980s a more contemporary R&B sound world had developed which combines elements of funk, dance, rhythm and blues and hip hop. 'I just called to say I love you' is a contrasting piece by Wonder which shows this change in musical genre.

The piece has a more relaxed nature when compared to 'Superstition' owing to the lush string synths and lack of rhythmic groove or horn section, using subtle melodic syncopation in the vocal line. An opening sustained Db major chord with bass alternating between tonic and dominant every two beats acts as a 4-bar introduction before the verse starts with a simple melody outlining dominant – tonic via the leading note, giving a yearning quality. The drum beat is programmed using a drum machine and the entire piece has an iconic 1980s sound. In a similar way to 'Superstition', the vocal lines use short phrases with an ascending profile, but rather than being pentatonic in construction the melody has a wider compass. Harmonically, the verse is rooted in the tonic Db with a chord sequence which also includes the dominant Ab and the secondary dominant Ebm. The harmonic rhythm is slow in the verses, with chords usually being settled on for several bars at a time.

In contrast, the chorus moves to a faster harmonic rhythm with one chord per bar (Ebm – Ab – Db – Db). On the second line of the chorus, a Bbm chord is introduced (the relative minor – 'care') replacing the tonic chord and giving an interrupted cadence. Wonder then repeats the chorus, moving up a semitone to D major, then again to Eb major, before an instrumental section which repeats the entire process using vocalise in the lyrics, giving a computerised sound effect.

For the final repetition in Eb major, Wonder's melody competes with the vocalise which now act as backing vocals in the gaps of the main melody. A short coda using a 2-bar sequence initiates a harmonic change, using Cb major and Db major (sus2) chords which then resolve back to the (new) tonic Eb major.

Both of these pieces demonstrate how one artist can encompass different musical styles throughout a career, as well as showing how musical genres achieve contrast by development of the styles which have come before them.

AoS2 KEY TERMS: A SUMMARY

Melody: riff, pitch bend, melisma, syllabic, hook, slide, glissando, ostinato, blue notes

Harmony/Tonality: power chords, sus4 chords, chord extensions/symbols, complex chords, tonic and dominant pedal, modes, pentatonic, blues scale

Structure: Intro/outro, middle 8, bridge, breakdown, verse, chorus, instrumental, break, drum fill, fade in/fade out

Timbre: studio effects, instruments and use, vocal timbres, instrumental techniques/effects

Texture: looping, layering, a cappella

Tempo, metre and rhythm: bpm, metronome mark, groove, backbeat, irregular metre

Music for media

Introduction

Music for media is a wonderfully exciting Area of Study that looks at the intricate relationship between music and action.

There are five named artists in this AoS for you to listen to, study and gain a critical appreciation of. Through detailed study of their music, you should seek to discover how their music confirms, suggests, questions and ultimately supports the unfolding drama.

This AoS looks at music especially composed for film, television and gaming, from 1958 to the present.

- Bernard Herrmann
- Hans Zimmer
- Michael Giacchino
- Thomas Newman
- Nobuo Uematsu

You are encouraged to answer the questions in this revision guide to aid your listening skills and learn more about essay technique. Some of the key vocabulary for this AoS is duplicated in other AoS; check your knowledge and develop your understanding by completing the exercises presented in the chapters on these other AoS, developing your musical ear.

The AQA AS Music specification can be found at www.aqa.org.uk/ subjects/music/as-and-a-level/music-7271. This contains a full list of the relevant vocabulary for each AoS. Further examples and explanations can be found in the *AQA AS and A Level Music Study Guide* (Rhinegold Education).

Musical language for this Area of Study

Timbre and Sonority

Given the nature of this AoS, many instruments are used in specific ways to convey particular meaning. It is vital that you have a working knowledge of the terms which follow, as well as examples of where such devices have been used and to what effect. Consider adding to the table below and making this part of your musical glossary.

By creating your own musical glossary, similar to the one at the back of this revision guide, you will be able to cross reference quickly where musical devices occur, allowing for more effective revision.

Instrument	Technique	Used in	Effect
String Section	Glissando (up)	Herrmann – *Psycho* 'The Murder'	Screeching, stabbing, alarm, high tessitura, dissonant D♯/E
Brass Section			
Woodwind Section			
Percussion Section			

Ensure you understand why the named artist uses the instruments they have chosen and what the effect of this is on the image on screen.

Harmonic analysis

Having completed the harmonic analysis questions in AoS2 (see page 48), complete the chords on the next page: these use Roman numerals rather than chord symbols, developing your understanding.

I+   vi   V   V7d   Ib   IV   V7   I

Complex chords

Composers in this genre use many types of advanced chord to create
a suitable picture for the action on screen. Complete the table below
(in C major for ease of comparison) for some of these advanced chords,
using the musical examples you have studied.

Chord	Symbol	Notation	Example
Augmented triad C – E – G♯	C^+		Herrmann – *Psycho 'Prelude'*
Added 6th chord	C^6		
Diminished triad			
Diminished 7th			
Half diminished 7th			

AoS3 MUSICAL LANGUAGE

Structural considerations

Diegetic music is music which can be heard by the characters on screen – i.e. it comes from a source within the character's world. Music from instruments which are in the film (i.e. a string quartet seen playing on stage) is called **source music.**

Non-Diegetic music is music which is not present in the action on screen – i.e. the characters on screen cannot hear it. This might be **underscore** if played quietly under a scene to help establish a mood or emotional state.

Mickey-mousing is an important structural consideration which ensures that the action on screen and the music are synchronised, with specific cues or hit-points giving moments of action. This is sometimes called parallel scoring.

Melodic devices

The most common melodic device used in this AoS is that of the **leitmotif** – the name given to a fragment of music that represents a specific character, event or emotion. These motifs enable the music to achieve a sense of unity and development, rather than new material being constantly required.

LEITMOTIF

One of the most famous (and most thrilling) uses of leitmotif in film music is the simple semitone figure by John Williams representing the shark 'Jaws'. Starting slow, quiet and distant in the low strings, Williams portrays the approaching shark by shortening the rests between the motif, adding a gradual crescendo and developing the tessitura by including higher instruments, until finally we see the shark. The music here is entirely responsible for building suspense.

STUDY PIECE

Hans Zimmer, *The Dark Night Rises* – 'Why so serious'

You can find this piece here: http://bit.ly/DarkKnightSuite, and here: http://bit.ly/DarkKnightScene

Evoking electronica, the music for Heath Ledger's iconic Joker uses a range of specific timbres and sudden dynamic contrasts to represent the tortured world of the character, including using razor blades on the strings of the instruments. Listen to the music in the link, then watch the corresponding scene. How does Zimmer's music picture the character of the Joker? Consider use of timbre, dynamics, structural devices and rhythm in your response.

Start by making a table to plan your response, adding to what has been started below. Be sure to give examples linking to the action on screen (e.g. speech, timing, bar number if using a score) in your full response.

Timbre	Dynamics	Structure	Rhythm	Effect
Electronic cello, guitar...	*piano* underscore...	non-diegetic music...	pedal points, additive...	unhinged, unpredictable, tortured...

Listening (Section A)

There will be four pieces to listen to and answer questions on in this part of the paper.

Here is a sample Section A of the exam paper covering AoS3.

Track 1 – Hans Zimmer, *The Lion King* 'King of Pride Rock'

Listen to this track, which you can find here: http://bit.ly/KingOfPrideRock

Extract: 1:00-1:24

1. Which orchestral instrument plays the opening melody?   [1 mark]

2. What is the time signature of the extract?   [1 mark]

3. Which graphic score best represents the opening melody? Select one answer.

a.

b.

c.

d.

[1 mark]

4. What is the quickest note value heard in the main melodic line? Select one answer.

Minim   **Crotchet**   **Quaver**   **Semiquaver**   [1 mark]

5. The tonic of the extract is C minor. On what chord does the extract end? Select one answer.

Tonic   **Dominant**   **Submediant**   **Relative Major**   [1 mark]

[Total: 5 marks]

Track 2 – Nobuo Uematsu, *Lost Odyssey* '103 The Gun Barrel Battle'

Listen to this track, which you can find here: http://bit.ly/UematsuLostOdyssey

Extract: 0:00-1:00

1. What is the tonality of this extract?   [1 mark]

2. Which one of these can be heard in the extract?

Trill   **Mordent**   **Acciaccatura**   **Hemiola**   [1 mark]

3. Which score best represents the rhythm of the percussion part?

a.

b.

c.

d.   [1 mark]

4. On the second repetition of the main theme, the strings are joined by which instrumental family?   [1 mark]

5. Towards the end of the extract, what harmonic device can be heard?

9-8 suspension   **Tierce de Picardie**

ascending sequence   **tonic pedal**   [1 mark]

[Total: 5 marks]

Track 3 – Bernard Herrmann, *North by Northwest* 'The Crash'

Listen to this track, which you can find here: http://bit.ly/HerrmannCrash, track 22

Extract: 7:28-8:28

The extract is taken from a film scene where a crop-duster plane is actively chasing a character before it spirals out of control and crashes into flames.

Explain how the use of musical elements enhances the audience's understanding of the scene.   [10 marks]

This is an extended response question requiring clarity of structure. Go through the elements in turn to create a coherent answer.

Essay question (Section C)

In the examination, you have to answer **one** essay question. There will be only one set for each AoS, so there is no choice beyond which AoS you have studied. You have 45 minutes to write the essay which is marked out of 30.

See page 55 for more information on essay writing and assessment.

Here follow two essays using the same title and the same musical examples. Use these as a comparison to help your own essay writing style.

Task: Essay Analysis

1. Read the essay by Candidate A below, marking it to the AQA mark scheme.

2. Where has the candidate gained marks? Where have marks been lost?

3. What can you learn from this candidate to prepare you for your exam?

4. Repeat points 1-3 for Candidate B's essay.

5. Check the comments on these essays in the Answers section at the back of the book.

Candidate A

Compare two contrasting passages from a film, TV or gaming score that you have studied and show how the named composer has enhanced the action on screen.

'Gladiator' is an epic story about a gladiator who is wronged and tries to get vengeance from the Roman emperor who has wronged him and killed his family. Maximus is denied his place as leader of the empire by the ambitious son of the dead emperor who kills his family. He is then captured by slavers and forced to fight as a gladiator by the slave masters. Because he was in the military and is a good fighter Maximus wins each local competition, eventually going to Rome to compete in the Colosseum where he battles lots of well known fighters. The emperor, jealous of Maximus' fighting, challenges him to a duel to put the threat to his throne down, but decides to stab him in the torso to throw the fight in his favour. However, Maximus ultimately wins the fight and kills the emperor.

The first piece of music I would like to talk about comes from the opening battle scene. The music is in D minor and sometimes changes to the relative major G major. The melody goes A-D-E-F which has a minor 6th interval and sounds sad. However, the strings make the music sound majestic which suits the Roman army. About a minute in, we realise that Maximus' peace deal to the Barbarians has been rejected and preparation for battle starts. A male voice sings a creepy melodic line using semitones and then the music gets faster and louder making it more excited. Herrmann then copies Holst's Mars by writing in $\frac{5}{4}$ and using motor rhythms, and was later sued for plagiarism. Trumpets and drums are used to make it sound like a battle. Trills and crescendos add interest. As the battle starts the main theme comes back to remind us it is the main theme and cross rhythms make the piece sound angry and scary. As the battle is won by the Roman soldiers the music moves to C major using pedal points. It does not sound too happy though as, even though the Romans won the battle, many of them died. There is a modal ending Em–Am.

The contrasting piece of music comes from the end of the film as Maximus dies in the Colosseum. It is in ternary form ABA and has an additive rhythm using primary chords. It is in A major with a dominant pedal – which continues even on chord 4 as a dissonant note. The vocal melody is ornamented and sometimes uses push rhythms to anticipate the beat, showing a sense of excitement. The B section has the main tune of C# F# A and then a big jump down to a B which is emotional. It is in F#m the relative minor and has some bare fifth chords. The A section then repeats the same as before.

To conclude these are two different bits of the film where the music is important to the audience.

Candidate B

Compare two contrasting passages from a film, TV or gaming score that you have studied and show how the named composer has enhanced the action on screen.

Hans Zimmer's music to Gladiator greatly enhances the visual plot, using leitmotif, ethnic instruments and driving rhythms to support the on screen action. The opening 'battle scene' and closing 'now we are free' are both action scenes with minimal dialogue, allowing the non-diegetic music to come to the fore in supporting and enhancing the plot.

The battle scene opens with the main theme, a 4 bar long majestic rising D minor idea spanning a minor 6th (A-D-E-F) performed on the horns with gentle percussive ostinato accompaniment. This theme is of utmost importance to the film, acting as a leitmotif throughout and, importantly, appearing at the very end of the film. A modulation to the relative major, F major, and use of dominant pedal (on C) allows for a subtle development of the idea. Greater use of chords complete with 4-3 and 9-8 suspensions and a rising chromatic violin line allows for the music to move towards a change in the scene, as Maximus, the central protagonist of the film, answers the Barbarian call for war and declares 'unleash hell'. The music suitably follows suit with an immediate change in temperature. A male voice replaces the alto female vocals heard at the very start of the film, using increased chromaticism in his nonsense syllables (F-E-F-G#), with the dissonance of the G# helping to move away from the diatonic landscape. The regular ostinato figures presented up to this point are avoided, matching the unpredictable tension of the plot.

As the build to battle commences, the music gains energy from an increase in tempo with the chromatic male vocal line now presented as an ostinato in the lower strings complete with brass hunting calls and bass pedal points. Cross-rhythms, accented weak beats and even a temporary move to $\frac{5}{4}$ time (evoking Holst's Mars) all give a sense of excitement and action to the plot, creating a victorious second theme. String trills, surging crescendo and dramatic twists with fragments of melodic material create anxiety – the Barbarians are putting up a good fight despite the Roman army being better prepared.

A tonal shift to C major and to $\frac{3}{4}$ time, complete with the opening leitmotif, marks a turning point in the battle, even though the action on screen continues unabated despite the slow motion effect.

The expansive use of strings using dotted minims, with dominant pedal points which resolve to the submediant rather than the tonic, gives a feeling of space and suspensions, including the Lydian #4-3, evoke feelings of loss. The driving second theme, central to the battle, remains absent, and the scene ends on a bare 5th A chord, suggesting the battle is far from over despite the apparent Roman victory.

'Now we are free' comes from the very end of the film, with Maximus ultimately dying having won the moral victory over the corrupt emperor. The injured Maximus is shifting in and out of consciousness, and as such the music is suitably dream-like, referencing the rural sounds and themes heard at the very start of the film. Constant quavers, played on a guitar sound effect, anchor a harmonic rhythm of 1 chord per bar. Despite the resolution in the plot, the tonic chord of A major often lacks resolution owing to the dominant pedal (on E) which is even used against the subdominant, creating an unresolved sus9 chord. First and second inversions are used frequently to allow the bass to have an ascending profile within the primary chord sequence.

The B section of this ternary form has the opening leitmotif presented in a developed fashion – in a new key of F#m with use of a 3+3+2 quaver additive rhythm (C#-F#-A-B). The falling interval of a

7th helps to add emotional weight to the scene before the melody twists to end in A major. The repetition of the A section prioritises the emotive vocals of Lisa Gerrard, complete with freer tempo, vocal push-rhythms and 4-3 and 9-8 suspensions. This rhythmic device does not create excitement however, as it is the only part providing rhythmic continuity, with the other parts having reduced to semibreve movement. The final perfect cadence includes a lengthy 4-3 suspension with a note of anticipation, giving a final bare 5th A chord.

The music to both of these contrasting scenes is central to the communication of the plot to the audience; not only does the music link to the action on screen, it actively enhances it, evoking previous memories and looking forward in the unfolding plot.

AoS3 KEY TERMS: A SUMMARY

Melody: leitmotif

Harmony/Tonality: power chords, sus4 chords, chord extensions/symbols, complex chords, tonic and dominant pedal, tonal, atonal, modal

Structure: cue, underscore, soundtrack, mickey-mousing, source music, diegetic and non-diegetic music

Sonority/Timbre: standard orchestral and jazz, rock and pop instruments, electronic instruments, ethnic instruments, technological effects, tremolo

Texture: cluster, polarized texture, drone

Tempo, metre and rhythm: metronome mark, additive rhythm, cross rhythm, rhythmic layering

Music for theatre

Introduction

Broadway, the West End, and all the many theatres in between – this AoS looks at how music can be used to entertain audiences across the globe.

There are five named artists in this AoS for you to listen to, study and gain a critical appreciation of. Notice that the specification cites that this is defined as 'music composed to govern, enhance or support a theatrical conception from 1930 to the present'. Whilst *The Threepenny Opera* can be seen as being originally composed earlier than this, the first film was completed after this and so it can be used for the specification.

- Kurt Weill
- Richard Rodgers
- Stephen Sondheim
- Claude-Michel Schönberg
- Jason Robert Brown

Some of the key vocabulary for this AoS is shared with others; it is advisable to work through those exercises in the previous chapters *before* starting on the work in this chapter to help develop your musical skills fully.

The AQA AS Music specification can be found at www.aqa.org.uk/subjects/music/as-and-a-level/music-7271. This contains a full list of the relevant vocabulary for each AoS. Further examples and explanations can be found in the *AQA AS and A Level Music Study Guide* (Rhinegold Education).

STUDY PIECE 1

Kurt Weill, *Lady in the Dark*
'The Saga of Jenny'

This exercise requires access to a score of the piece which cannot be reproduced here for copyright reasons. It can be purchased online from Musicnotes, where the main features of the song are notated clearly.

Introduction ('There once was a girl named Jenny')

Consider the first part of the song and mark up your score. You may wish to differentiate between musical elements when writing your ideas down to aid revision.

Melody:

- If the sung melody is **syllabic** or **melismatic**
- Any **portamento** use (vocal **glissando**) – whether notated or completed in performance
- Any intervals of importance (e.g. because of their repetition)
- Is the melody **conjunct** or **disjunct**? Are there any specific (angular) jumps?

Rhythm:

- Any rhythms of importance and why these might occur

Harmony:

- Any chord extensions (6th, 7th, 9th, 11th, 13th and so on) and how these are voiced
- Any chromatic harmony (such as diminished 7th chords, augmented chords) or chromatic countermelodies
- Any passing **modulations** (look out for the new leading note as an accidental)

Tempo:

- What tempo the piece is – spotting if it changes and what the metronome mark is

Texture:

- The role of the (structural) chorus and instrumental backing

Verse ('Jenny made her mind up')

The bluesy character of the song is clearly noticeable here, with some idiomatic touches. Continue marking up your score, using the note-taking system you used for the introduction.

- Establish the tonic key of the verse. Highlight any **blue notes** in the melody, looking out for ♯4th/♭5th and ♭7th. Are these used on any particular words?
- Analyse the chord sequence; which chords are not closely related to the tonic key?
- What is the role of the following instruments in this section? Highlight your findings on your score.
  - Drum kit
  - Bass
  - Violins
  - Brass

Chorus ('Poor Jenny, bright as a penny')

The centre of the song, this 9-bar section combines regular 4-bar phrasing with a short instrumental link to return to the verse. Consider the following:

- Which chords are not closely related to the tonic? Why are they used?
- Are any **suspensions** used? If so, where are they used and why are they used at that point?
- Are there any distinctive rhythms used? Are these developed?
- How does the line 'she lost one dad and mother' relate to 'a sister and a brother'?
- Are there any features of **word painting**?

Bridge ('Jenny points a moral')

This acts as the final section of the song, balancing the repetition of the verse and chorus to provide the listener with something new. Compare this section with the music that has come before, thinking about:

- Melody: the **tessitura**, use of rhythms, use of **sequence**
- Tonality: there is a **modulation** into this section. From where to where? How?
- Harmony: how is this different to the music that has come before? How are **blues notes** used, especially in the final 2 bars?
- Texture: how do the final eight bars change texturally? Link this to the role of the instruments

Approaching musical analysis in this way is a great way to get to know lots of musical detail about a piece of music, enabling you to write with musical conviction in the examination and improve your musical ear.

Aural analysis exercise

This alternative approach can be taken where a score is not available, using your ear to refine how the composer uses the musical elements in a piece of music by listening to the piece four times in total, focussing on different elements as you listen.

1st playing	■ **Sonority (Timbre):** number, type, family, relationship, special techniques? ■ **Tonality:** major, minor, modal, atonal? ■ **Rhythm:** time signature, tempo (bpm), metronome mark (mm) ■ **Structure:** do any sections repeat? Are they developed?
2nd playing	■ **Melody:** conjunct, disjunct, leitmotif, syllabic, melismatic, pitch bend ■ **Rhythm:** ostinato, riff ■ **Harmony:** chromatic chords, suspensions, chord extensions, cadences ■ **Tonality:** are there any modulations? Link to structure
3rd playing	■ **Harmony:** harmonic rhythm ■ **Melody:** articulation, phrase structure ■ **Texture:** changes, link to word painting, a cappella, colla voce ■ **Style:** period, plot, purpose
4th playing	■ **Confirm all points** above and add detail, making references to the structure and/or text

STUDY PIECE 2

Claude-Michel Schönberg, *Les Miserables* 'Empty Chairs at Empty Tables'

You can find this song here: http://bit.ly/EmptyChairsEmptyTables

Using the steps from the listening table above, listen to the music in the link and aurally analyse the piece of music in the boxes below.

Try to complete this work on your own, giving a few minutes between each performance. At the end, compare your work with that of your peers to facilitate a discussion. Add in any extra points they might have, then compare to the suggestions in the Answers section at the back of the book. How does your response compare?

1st playing	
2nd playing	
3rd playing	
4th playing	

REVISION REVIEW

Having completed both approaches, discuss with your peers which approach they preferred and why. Which approach yields the most detail for the purpose of writing an essay? How else might we approach analysing music?

Listening (Section A)

There will be four pieces to listen to and answer questions on in this part of the paper. Here is a sample Section A of the exam paper covering AoS4.

Track 1 – Claude-Michel Schönberg, *Miss Saigon* 'I still believe'

Listen to this song, which you can find here: http://bit.ly/MissSaigonISB

Extract: 0:15-1:09

1. What interval does the voice sing when it first starts?

   _____

   _____   [2 marks]

2. What is the tonality of the extract?

   Major   Minor   Atonal   Modal   [1 mark]

3. Underline **one** statement which is true about this extract.

   a. The vocal line is melismatic with no blue notes

   b. The vocal line is melismatic with blue notes

   c. The vocal line is syllabic with no blue notes

   d. The vocal line is syllabic with blue notes   [1 mark]

4. Which one of these harmonic devices is used in this extract?

   Circle of Fifths   Dominant Pedal

   Diminished 7th chord   Tierce de Picardie   [1 mark]

   [Total: 5 marks]

Track 2 – Richard Rodgers, *Oklahoma!* 'I cain't say no'

Listen to this song, which you can find here: http://bit.ly/CaintSayNo

Extract: 0:48-1:24

1   I'm jist a girl who cain't say no

2   I'm in a turrible fix

3   I always say 'come on, le's go'

4   Jist when I orta say nix!

5   When a person tries to kiss a girl

6   I know she orta give his face a smack

7   But as soon as someone kisses me

8   I somehow, sorta, wanta kiss him back!

1. What is the tempo of this song?

Presto   **Lento**   **Moderato**   **Andante**   [1 mark]

2. Underline **one** statement which is true about this extract.

    a. Lines 1 and 2 are the same as lines 3 and 4

    b. Line 2 and line 4 are different

    c. Line 1 and 3 are different

    d. Lines 1 and 3 are the same as lines 2 and 4   [1 mark]

3. Which one of these devices can be heard in this extract?

Sequence   **Ostinato**   **Circle of Fifths**   **Appoggiatura**   [1 mark]

4. Which term best describes the texture of this extract?

Antiphonal   **Monophonic**

Melody and Accompaniment   **Imitation**   [1 mark]

5. What interval does the voice sing in line 8 between 'him' and 'back'?

_____   [1 mark]

[Total: 5 marks]

Track 3 – Stephen Sondheim, *Sweeney Todd* 'Opening Ballad'

Listen to this song, which you can find here: http://bit.ly/SweeneyToddPrelude

Extract: 0:41-2:00

The extract is taken from the opening number of a show about a demonic, murdering barber in London.

Explain how the use of musical elements enhances the audience's understanding of the scene.   **[10 marks]**

Essay question (Section C)

In the examination, you have to answer one essay question. There will be only one set for each AoS so there is no choice beyond which AoS you have studied. You have 45 minutes to write the essay which is marked out of 30.

See page 55 for more information on essay writing and assessment.

Consider the essay question on the next page, planning your response before embarking on the writing process. Think about which musical examples will best allow you to respond to the question and then plan your response:

- **Introduction** – address the question, introduce the two pieces used to answer the question

- **Main Essay** – are you going to talk extensively about the first piece in one paragraph and the second in another? Or are you going to compare directly both pieces side by side, element by element? How might the wording of the question help you to decide?

- **Conclusion** – have you answered the question?

Having established your basic plan, give thought to your essay style. A good set of rules to follow are:

1. **Keep the introduction short**, reusing language from the question to help focus your argument on answering the question. Avoid excessive non-musical context which wastes precious time and struggles to be awarded marks.

2. Start each paragraph with a **short analytical point** which answers the question.

3. Back up this point with **evidence** from the music you have chosen.

4. Avoid simply describing the music, but instead give **analytical detail**, evaluating the effect of a particular musical device rather than simply stating its presence.

5. Start a new paragraph for a new point, following points 2-4.

6. Keep your conclusion short, addressing the question. Avoid simply repeating the points you have already made – try and save something new to say to give your essay a real sense of style.

Compare two songs by the same named artist which show contrasting emotional states. How has the artist achieved this in their music?

Introduction 1

'One Day More' and 'Empty Chairs at Empty Tables' are two contrasting songs from *Les Miserables*. The first ends the first act, with all the principal characters on stage, while the second is a sad lament sung as a solo.

Introduction 2

The two songs I have chosen to write about in this essay are 'One Day More' and 'Empty Chairs' from *Les Miserables* by Schonberg. They are contrasting songs; 'One Day More' is a chorus number which has a sense of hope for the unfolding drama and 'Empty Chairs' is a solo sung by Marius who is sad following the death of many of his friends. Schonberg uses the musical elements to make musical contrasts impacting the drama.

Introduction task

Read both introductions opposite; both contain relevant information, but could have a greater sense of essay style. Rewrite the introduction using this information and the guidance from pages 79-80. How does your introduction compare to that of your peers?

Writing the essay

The points in the table below are the musical features that could be used to write your essay. Using these points, write the essay, trying to follow style steps 1-6 from pages 79-80. When you have finished, mark your essay according to the mark scheme and compare it with your peers.

'One Day More'	'Empty Chairs at Empty Tables'
▪ Enticing, exciting, unfolding plot	▪ Melancholy, lonely, regret
▪ **Simultaneous quodlibet** – chorus each sing their respective melodic parts, combined.	▪ Solo Tenor, sotto voce
	▪ 32-bar song form (adapted)
▪ Epic tying together of musical motif	▪ A sections ('there's a grief') harmonically unadventurous (harmonic rhythm = 1 chord per bar)
▪ Through-composed A B C with linking bridge sections and coda	▪ B section ('at the table') faster harmonic rhythm (two chords per bar) and move to relative major C major
▪ C section presents all the different themes together	
▪ Coda – all sing 'who am I?'	
▪ A major (tonic) – **diatonic functional harmony**. Moves to Bm (bar 18), B major (bar 20), Fm (bar 26), **enharmonic pivot chords**	▪ Use of perfect cadences, extensions, 7ths, broken chords (9ths)
	▪ Modulates to C♯m (tertiary relationship to Am) – impact
▪ Perfect cadences at the end of sections	▪ Conjunct melody, falling through 5th, some **disjunct** moments
▪ Melody and accompaniment, increasingly **contrapuntal**, unison in coda. Final **homophonic** chords.	▪ Melody and accompaniment – **word painting** 'lonely barricade' as bass drops out
▪ Grand use of orchestra – brass interjections	▪ Constant quavers at close – movement and momentum

AoS4 KEY TERMS: A SUMMARY

Melody: pitch bend, melisma, syllabic, slide, glissando, leitmotif, angular

Harmony: power chords, sus4 chords, chord extensions, complex chords, chord symbols

Structure: intro/outro, bridge, verse, chorus, instrumental, middle 8

Sonority/Timbre: studio/technological effects, orchestral and contemporary instruments, vocal timbres, specific instrumental techniques

Texture: a cappella, colla voce

Tempo, metre and rhythm: bpm, metronome mark, irregular metre

Jazz

Introduction

From 'cool' to 'hot', the music of this Area of Study is richly rewarding.

There are six named artists in this AoS for you to listen to, study and gain a critical appreciation of. Notice that the specification cites that Jazz is defined as 'a style of music characterised by a strong but flexible rhythmic understructure with solo and ensemble improvisations on basic tunes and chord patterns and a highly sophisticated harmonic idiom from 1920 to the present'.

- Louis Armstrong
- Duke Ellington
- Charlie Parker
- Miles Davis
- Pat Metheny
- Gwilym Simcock

Some of the key vocabulary for this AoS is shared with others; it is advisable to work through the exercises in the previous chapters *before* starting on the work in this chapter to help develop your musical skills fully.

The AQA AS Music specification can be found at www.aqa.org.uk/subjects/music/as-and-a-level/music-7271. This contains a full list of the relevant vocabulary for each AoS. Further examples and explanations can be found in the *AQA AS and A Level Music Study Guide* (Rhinegold Education).

Jazz and Blues featured as an optional unit in the old AQA A Level (Unit 4); you may therefore find there are still resources online for that legacy specification which may be useful to develop your understanding.

Musical language for this Area of Study

Melodic features

Jazz is made by the improvisatory nature of the music, with a whole host of melodic devices being used. For the extracts below, consider which of the following melodic devices you can hear, writing in the box next to the extract:

- **Glissando**
- **Pitch-bend**
- **Smear**
- **Spill/fall-off**
- **Rip**
- **Mordent**
- **Triplet**
- **Ghost note**
- **Acciaccatura**

Extract 1	Charlie Parker, 'Confirmation' http://bit.ly/ CharlieParkerConfirmation
Extract 2	Miles Davis, 'Bye Bye Blackbird' http://bit.ly/ByeBlackbird, track 10
Extract 3	Louis Armstrong, 'When the Saints' http://bit.ly/ LouisArmstrongSolo

Blues scales

There are three principal types of **blues scale** – the **hexatonic** (6-note), **heptatonic** (7-note) and **nonatonic** (9-note). The description of each is given below.

Using this description, write in the correct accidentals on the score to match the description.

Hexatonic: 6-note scale

- Formed of a minor **pentatonic** scale
- Added ♯4th (sometimes notated as ♭5th)

Heptatonic: 7-note scale

- **Diatonic** scale
- Evokes the minor mode – minor 3rd, 5th and 7th

Nonatonic: 9-note scale

- **Diatonic** major scale with 2 additional notes
- Added minor 3rd
- Added minor 7th

Extended chords

Extended chords are made by adding notes to the basic major or minor triad.

Tonic (I) – Mediant (III) – Dominant (V) = Triad

The word 'mediant' comes from the Latin 'to be in the middle' – the third is in the middle of the tonic and dominant to make the triad.

AoS5 MUSICAL LANGUAGE

These added notes often go up in thirds from the dominant:

Tonic – Mediant – Dominant – 7th – 9th – 11th – 13th

If we use the scale of the chord we wish to extend, this gives us the notes we can use to extend the chord. These scales can include major or minor, or more complex patterns such as the seven musical **modes** or a **diminished** (**octatonic**) scale. The table below shows how these chords are constructed using this process, using the **mixolydian** mode.

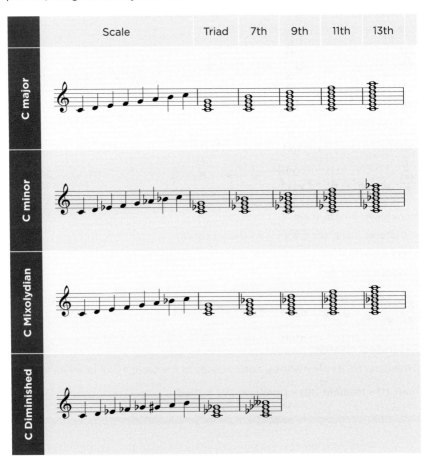

Chord Voicing

Working out the correct notes for the extended chord is the first part of the process. However, if you play the chords above they will probably not sound as exotic as similar chords used in jazz standards. This is to do with how the chord has been voiced – that is to say, how the chord is ordered, spaced and constructed.

A good example of this point is the opening bars of Miles Davis's 'Four':

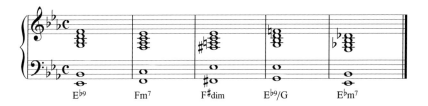

Notice how there is a sense of contrary motion between the top and bass of the chord, using **inversions**, extended chords and a **diminished** chord.

Experiment with voicing these extended chords in different ways. Why might Davis have voiced these chords in this way? If the tempo and style was more 'cool' jazz, how might the voicings have changed?

STUDY PIECE 1

Gwilym Simcock, 'Antics'
You can find this song here: http://bit.ly/AnticsGS

This is an energetic performance which is based on a central repeated riff with some highly virtuosic instrumental moments. As you listen to the piece, think about the way the instruments are being used and how they interact with each other in this original composition.

You may wish to complete a more extensive aural analysis of this piece; if so, consider using the approach outlined in the chapter for Area of Study 4 (page 75).

STUDY PIECE 2

Pat Metheny, 'Bright Size Life'

You can find this song here: http://bit.ly/BrightSizeLife

Structured loosely in an AABA **popular song form**, this iconic piece uses many features for which Metheny became famous, including guitar licks, chordal harmonies, extended chords and modal influences. How do the instruments in this piece interact with each other? How does this piece compare musically to the Simcock piece above?

Listening (Section A)

There will be four pieces to listen to and answer questions on in this part of the paper. Here is a sample Section A of the exam paper covering AoS5.

Track 1 – Louis Armstrong, 'West End Blues'

Listen to this track, which you can find here: http://bit.ly/WestEndBlues1928

Extract: 0:00-0:52

1. Which instrument starts this piece, playing an unaccompanied solo?

_____   [1 mark]

2. The full band enters and the Head starts at 0:16.
   Which note values does the piano play?

   Quavers   Crotchets   Minims   Semibreves   [1 mark]

3. Underline **one** statement which is true about this extract.

   a. The Head uses chords I, IV and V

   b. The Head uses chords I, II and V

   c. The Head uses chords I, IV and VI

   d. The Head uses chords I, III and V   [1 mark]

4. Which word best describes the clarinet part?

Tremolo   **Staccato**   **Chalumeau**   **Marcato**   [1 mark]

5. What technique is used in the trombone playing?

_____   [1 mark]

[Total: 5 marks]

Track 2 – Duke Ellington, 'Black and Tan Fantasy'

Listen to this track, which you can find here: http://bit.ly/BlackAndTanFantasy

Extract: 0:00-0:42

1. What melodic device can be heard in the opening trumpet and trombone melody?

_____   [1 mark]

2. What rhythmic device can be heard in the piano part?

Hemiola   **Syncopation**   **Cross rhythm**   **Polyrhythm**   [1 mark]

3. How has the tone of the brass instruments been altered?

_____   [1 mark]

4. What instrument enters playing the solo at 0:26?

Tenor Saxophone   **Alto Saxophone**

Clarinet   **Baritone Saxophone**   [1 mark]

5. What melodic device can be heard at the end of the extract?

Ascending sequence   **Descending sequence**

Appoggiatura   **Drone**   [1 mark]

[Total: 5 marks]

Track 3 – Miles Davis, 'All Blues'

Listen to this track, which you can find here: http://bit.ly/AllBluesMilesDavis

Extract: 0:00-0:53

1. What is the interval in the opening riff played by the alto saxophone and tenor saxophone?

   _____   [1 mark]

2. What is the time signature of the extract?

   $\frac{2}{4}$ $\frac{4}{4}$ $\frac{5}{4}$ $\frac{6}{4}$ [1 mark]

3. What interval is played by the trumpet when it first plays?

   4th   5th   6th   7th   [1 mark]

4. State how the snare drum is played in the extract.

   _____   [1 mark]

5. What term best describes the harmony of this extract?

   Major   Minor   Atonal   Modal   [1 mark]

   [Total: 5 marks]

Track 4 – Charlie Parker, 'A Night in Tunisia'

Listen to this track, which you can find here: http://bit.ly/TunisiaCharlieParker

Extract: 0:50-2:16

What elements of Bebop can be heard in this extract?   [10 marks]

Essay question (Section C)

In the examination, you have to answer one essay question. There will be only one set for each AoS, so there is no choice beyond which AoS you have studied. You have 45 minutes to write the essay which is marked out of 30.

See page 55 for more information on essay writing and assessment.

Consider the essay title below, planning your response to it. The first section of the essay, looking at Miles Davis's 'Four', has been started. Write an introduction, then a second section using a contrasting piece by Miles Davis, and a conclusion to finish. If you have time, you can also rewrite the first paragraph to add more detail addressing the question.

Choosing one of the named artists, comment on how their music has achieved stylistic variety. You should refer to two contrasting pieces of music discussing instrumentation, harmony and melody, as appropriate.

Miles Davis 'Four'

Written for a jazz quintet (trumpet, tenor sax, piano, bass and drum kit) the 1964 recording of 'Four' exemplifies Davis' reworking of his earlier Bebop style, using a fast tempo and some exceptionally complex instrumental writing. These include a fast walking bass on the double bass, played pizzicato, and very fast comping on the piano using a variety of extended chords. The drum kit also has some virtuosic moments with fast ride cymbal rhythms and occasional rim shots. The harmonic vocabulary is complex, as expected for the genre of Jazz. Whilst the basic harmonic progression could be analysed in a simplistic fashion (the opening four bars, for example, could be seen as being in the tonic Eb major), it is Davis' use of substitution chords and extensions which make the harmonic language complex. This includes the chromatic Eb9 – Fm7 – F#° – Eb9/G (first inversion) – Ebm7 of the opening which effectively moves to the tonic minor at the end of the 4-bar phrase as well as a similar chromatic movement from Gm7 – F#m7 – Fm7 – Bb7 which follows. This gives a standard ii-V turnaround to allow the main idea to start again. Davis uses sequences and improvisation in the melody, with the choruses having a wider range.

AOS5 KEY TERMS: A SUMMARY

Melody: glissando, pitch-bend, smear, spill/fall-off, rip

Harmony: chord extensions, added note chords, substitution (including tritone substitution), jazz symbols, turn-around

Tonality: blue notes, blues scale, pentatonic scale, octatonic (diminished) scale, modes

Structure: 12-bar blues, chord changes, song form/standard form, middle 8/bridge, intro/outro, head, chorus, fours, break

Sonority/Timbre: growl/talking trumpet, harmon mute, wah-wah mute, ghosted notes, slap bass, rim-shot, standard big-band instruments

Texture: a cappella, heterophonic

Tempo, metre and rhythm: swing and straight rhythm, cross rhythms, push and drag, double time, ametrical, riff, stop time

Contemporary traditional music

Introduction

Taking something old and making it into something new is a cornerstone of artistic endeavour. This Area of Study takes an ethnomusicological approach to five different musical fusions.

There are five named artists in this AoS for you to listen to, study and gain a critical appreciation of. The specification cites that music in this genre is defined as 'music influenced by traditional musical features fused with contemporary elements and styles'.

- Astor Piazzolla
- Toumani Diabaté
- Anoushka Shankar
- Mariza
- Bellowhead

As with the previous AoS, the exercises in this chapter will help with specific revision as well as helping to develop your general musicianship.

The AQA AS Music specification can be found at www.aqa.org.uk/subjects/music/as-and-a-level/music-7271. This contains a full list of the relevant vocabulary for each AoS. Further examples and explanations can be found in the *AQA AS and A Level Music Study Guide* (Rhinegold Education).

Contemporary v traditional

With this AoS it is vital to understand how the named artists are using traditional musical ideas in a more contemporary way. Below are examples of how you could approach this revision.

Tango and Piazzolla

Piazzolla is credited by many musicologists as being the father of *Tango Nuevo* ('new tango'), taking an older tradition and adding new ideas to it. In Piazzolla's own words, 'my tango does meet the present'.

Traditional elements ('tango')	Contemporary elements ('tango nuevo')
■ $\frac{4}{4}$ time ■ use of accents, including on weak beats ■ **syncopation** ■ **ostinato** – often 3+3+2 quavers ■ melancholy – minor key ■ strong dynamic contrasts ■ a singer often features – sad lyrics ■ bass often playing on beats 4 and 1	Based on traditional tango, but: ■ singer avoided – instrumental (sometimes including electric guitar and drum kit) ■ greater influence from jazz and later rock/pop music ■ Chromatic extensions ■ specific instrumental techniques to achieve new timbral colours

String techniques

Listen to one of Piazzolla's most famous pieces, *Libertango*, and see if you can hear these more contemporary features. You can find it here: http://bit.ly/LibertangoAP

Extract: 0:00 – 2:46

Listen out for:

■ Use of semitonal **auxiliary notes** in the main melody

■ The minor tonality with unexpected **modulations**

■ The use of **additive rhythms** – 3+3+2 permeating the texture with cross-rhythms

■ Use of **pitch bends** in the melody

■ The way the instruments are played – e.g. stab chords on the bandoneon

The use of instruments in specific ways – particularly stringed instruments – is central to Piazzolla's sound world. The specification requires you to have a working knowledge of these. Revise these terms by listening to the extracts and completing the table below:

Name	Evidence	Description
Chicharra	http://bit.ly/ Chicharra	
Latigo	http://bit.ly/ TangoLatigo	
Arrastre	http://bit.ly/ Arrastre	
Tambor	http://bit.ly/ TangoTambor	
Golpe de Caja	http://bit.ly/ GalopeDeCaja	

An excellent guide to string techniques can be found at http://bit.ly/StringTechniquesLSO where some members of the LSO guide you through various different playing techniques. This would also be invaluable for composition work.

Fado and Mariza

The Fado tradition has many similarities with tango, and artists have also been quick to take the tradition and add a contemporary twist. Mariza has brought the tradition to a more global audience by combining the traditions of Fado with Iberian pop music.

The following two pieces show the traditional and the contemporary for Fado. As you listen to them, consider how they are similar and different, completing a table to show your working. A few starting points are given here:

STUDY PIECE 1

Traditional – Argentina Santos, 'Maria Severa'

Listen to this track, which you can find here: http://bit.ly/MariaSevera

Listen for the traditional ensemble using Portuguese guitars; the fluctuations between major and minor chords; and drama added with tempo changes at the end of each verse.

STUDY PIECE 2

Contemporary – Mariza, 'Alma'

Listen to this track, which you can find here: http://bit.ly/MarizaAlma

Consider the influence of Iberian pop music – the modern production techniques; the use of pop conventions; the regularity of tempo, $\frac{4}{4}$ time and harmonic rhythm.

English folk music and Bellowhead

Famous for reviving the English folk tradition, Bellowhead take traditional folk pieces including sea shanties, jigs and songs and put a contemporary focus on them.

In a similar way to the Mariza exercise above, listen to one of Bellowhead's songs, comparing the traditional with the contemporary. The example opposite, using the sea shanty tradition, can be used to help you with your independent analysis.

Traditional – Roll Alabama Roll http://bit.ly/RollAlabama	Bellowhead – Roll Alabama http://bit.ly/BellowheadRoll Alabama
- Solo/chorus in **call and response** - Male vocal chorus use title of song - Soloist tells the story - **Diatonic, functional harmony** including perfect cadences - Repetitive phrases – 4 bar - Fiddle solo - Verse 1 **a cappella** voices - Verse 2 instrumental accompaniment - Verse 3 fiddle **countermelody**	- Faster tempo - Fiddle melody interacts with soloist with chorus calls from verse 1 - Four-on-the-floor drum beat - Repetitive phrases – 4 bar - Fragmented instrumental entries - Word painting/textural reduction - **Cross rhythms**

Listening (Section A)

There will be four pieces to listen to and answer questions on in this part of the paper. Here is a sample Section A of the exam covering AoS6.

Track 1 – Anoushka Shankar and Norah Jones, 'Unsaid'

Listen to this song, which you can find here: http://bit.ly/UnsaidASNJ

Extract: 0:00-1:04

1. Which instrument plays the solo line in the introduction?

_____   [1 mark]

2. Which term below best describes the tempo of the song?

   Allegro   **Moderato**   **Adagio**   **Presto**   [1 mark]

3. Underline **one** statement which is true about this extract.

a. The piece is in $\frac{4}{4}$ and changes to $\frac{2}{4}$ at the end of the extract

b. The piece is in $\frac{3}{4}$ and changes to $\frac{4}{4}$ at the end of the extract

c. The piece is in $\frac{6}{8}$ and changes to $\frac{4}{4}$ at the end of the extract

d. The piece is in $\frac{4}{4}$ and changes to $\frac{3}{4}$ at the end of the extract   [1 mark]

4. Which melodic device is used in the solo instrumental part?

_____   [1 mark]

5. When the voice starts, what chord sequence is used twice?
Select **one** answer from the list below.

a.   D   Bm   Gm   D   ☐

b.   D   Bm   A   Em   ☐

c.   D   F♯m   Bm   D   ☐

d.   D   A   F♯m   A   ☐   [1 mark]

[Total: 5 marks]

Track 2 – Diabaté, 'Solo'

Listen to this song, which you can find here: http://bit.ly/KoraSolo

Extract: 0:00-1:05

1. Which instrument plays the solo line at the start of the song?

_____   [1 mark]

2. Two intervals are heard at the start of this song.
Name the missing interval.

Major 2nd (C-D) and _____   [1 mark]

3. After this opening riff, the music changes to include which one
of the following?

Triplets   Swung rhythms   Syncopation   Hemiola   [1 mark]

4. A melody enters over this accompaniment. Which **two** terms best describe this melody?

Ascending   **Descending**   **Additive Rhythm**

Syncopation   **Circle of Fifths**   **Mordent**   [2 marks]

[**Total: 5 marks**]

Track 3 – Bellowhead, 'London Town'

Listen to this song, which you can find here:
http://bit.ly/BellowheadLondonTown

Extract for this exam paper: 0:00-0:56

1. Which instrument plays chords in the opening?

_____   [1 mark]

2. Which device best describes the rhythm of the opening?

Syncopated   **Four-on-the-floor**   **Tala**   **Polyrhythm**   [1 mark]

3. Four chords are used in the introduction. Select the option below which is correct.

a. I   VI   IV   V   ☐

b. I   II   V   V   ☐

c. I   V   IV   I   ☐

d. I   IV   VI   V   ☐   [1 mark]

4. The drums enter at 0:40. On which **two** beats does the snare play?

_____ and _____   [2 marks]

[**Total: 5 marks**]

AoS6 SECTION C

Track 4 – Piazzolla, 'Knife Fight'

Listen to this piece, which you can find here: http://bit.ly/PiazzollaKnifeFight

Extract: 0:00-1:53

The excerpt is called 'Knife Fight'. How are the elements of music used to evoke this title?   [10 marks]

Essay question (Section C)

In the examination, you have to answer one essay question. There will be only one set for each AoS so there is no choice beyond which AoS you have studied. You have 45 minutes to write the essay which is marked out of 30.

See page 55 for more information on essay writing and assessment.

For a named artist you have studied, discuss how they have developed a traditional style for a contemporary audience.

This is a fairly standard question for this AoS, and certainly one you need to practise and be able to address fully. It is also an excellent question to approach for revision for each of the named artists. Anoushka Shankar is covered in the sample assessment material on the AQA website, so the essay here looks at a different named artist.

Sample assessment papers showing how the exam will be laid out and practice questions can be found on the AQA website at www.aqa.org. uk/subjects/music/as-and-a-level/music-7271/assessment-resources

As you approach this essay, remember the guidance given in the previous chapters which have discussed approaches to writing the essay as well as looking at how to style your work.

Indicative content: Astor Piazzolla

Born in Argentina, 1921. Fused Argentine Tango with Jazz and Classical music to create 'tango nuevo' – new tango.

'Milonga del Ángel' http://bit.ly/MilongaDelAngelAP	'Yo soy Maria' http://bit.ly/YoSoyMaria
■ Milonga – from the slow tempo tradition ■ **Ternary form** ABA + Intro ■ **Habanera rhythm** outlining tonic/dominant in bass ■ Use of C♯ in violin – **pitch bending**, use of sul G ■ Bandoneon solo (crescendo) ■ Repeat changes – violin high octave ■ Improvised feel ■ **Syncopation** ■ Instrument techniques – bellow vibrato on bandoneon, **glissando** in double bass	■ Bass habanera rhythm 3+3+2 quavers A-F-E ■ **Additive rhythms** and **cross rhythms** ■ Falling profile of melody (E-A) ■ **Semitonal auxiliaries** including moving the top note earlier in the repeat ■ Chromatically altering melody to fit chord – D♯/augmented 2nd interval ■ **Circle of fifths** ■ Unexpected chords – e.g. Fm exploring flat side harmony ■ String techniques ■ Move from Am to B♭m to Bm – semitone rise/raise temperature

Born in Argentina in 1921, Piazzolla reworked ideas found in Argentine tango to create a contemporary aspect of the form. By fusing the traditional form with more contemporary ideas found in jazz and twentieth-century classical music, he created a new type of tango – 'tango nuevo' – which he described by saying 'my tango does meet the present'. Two pieces that show these traditional and contemporary features are 'Milonga del Angel' and 'Yo soy Maria'.

'Milonga del Angel' combines the traditional and contemporary from the outset. Milonga is a significant word in tango, linking to an event or place where tango is danced as well as a type of music which is often of fast tempo in $\frac{2}{4}$ time. Piazzolla reworks this tradition by writing a slow tempo piece in $\frac{4}{4}$. The piece is in ternary form with a short introduction, with Piazzolla's traditional free approach to tonal scheme. While the introduction and opening A section are based around the tonic B minor, the B section modulates more widely including moves to Em, F#m and Cm – the flattened second degree. The repeat of the A section moves even further away from the tonic, traversing through G#m and Fm.

Further evidence of traditional tango can be found in Piazzolla's rhythmic choices. He employs the traditional habanera rhythm and shape in the bass (outlining tonic and dominant using a dotted rhythm and octave jump on beats 3 and 4) as well as syncopation. His choice of instruments – solo violin and bandoneon with accompaniment – is also traditional, with some more contemporary touches including vibrato on the bandoneon bellows, glissando on the bass and exploiting the full range of the violin in its countermelody – sul G, pitch bends creating expressive sus2 chords, and very high registers to contrast on the repeat.

Next steps

Now consider writing the second half of the essay to reference 'Yo soy Maria', using the indicative content outline above. Finally, write your conclusion. Mark your work to the mark scheme, comparing yours with that of your peers.

AoS6 KEY TERMS: A SUMMARY

Melody: raga, pitch bend, kumbengo (ostinato riffs on kora), birmintingo (improvised runs)

Harmony: drone, sus4 chords, chord symbols, added note chords

Tonality: specific modes

Structure: tango nuevo, milonga, fado, alap, fusion, verse/chorus, folk rock, song form/standard form

Sonority/Timbre: specific instruments, specific string techniques, studio effects, piano glissando, drone, sitar sympathetic strings

Texture: looping, layering, heterophonic

Tempo, metre and rhythm: polyrhythm, Latin 3+3+2 rhythm (additive), habanera rhythm, tala, riff

PERFORMANCE

Performance and composition: coursework components

As well as the final Appraising Music (Component 1) examination, you must also complete two coursework units, in Performance (Component 2) and Composition (Component 3).

Performance

This unit is worth 30% of the total marks at AS Level; regular practice, keen research into your music and a willingness to listen to constructive criticism are all key attributes to producing a successful recital.

PERFORMING REQUIREMENTS

Minimum duration: 6 minutes

Options:

- Acoustic performance – solo and/or ensemble; instrumental and/or vocal

OR

- IT Production – presented to AQA in the form of a recording with a score, lead sheet or guide recording (if the former is unavailable).

Remember to ensure that your instrumental teacher is fully up to speed with the requirements for the unit; it has its own marking criteria which need to be fully understood to access the highest marks.

While planning your final recital is important, it is not the only performance-based activity you should be doing during the course. Consider playing through your composition work to establish if ideas are idiomatic and full of musical character. Also try out on your instrument the ideas you learn through your musical analysis.

Composition

This unit is also worth 30% of the marks at AS Level. You will be awarded for creative use of the musical elements, showing a strong musical technique and a keen awareness of musical development.

COMPOSING REQUIREMENTS

You must complete two separate compositions:

- Composition 1: composition to a brief set by AQA
- Composition 2: free composition

Combined, your compositions should last a minimum of 4½ minutes; any submissions falling below this minimum time will not be awarded any marks.

In-depth advice on the Performing and Composing tasks is available in the *AQA AS and A Level Music Study Guide* (Rhinegold Education).

Answers

AoS1 : Western Classical tradition 1650-1910

Pages 9-10: Exercise 1 – Contours

Description	Bar number(s)
An ascending scalic contour	1
A descending scalic contour	7
An ascending arpeggio contour	2
A descending arpeggio contour	8
A triadic contour	5
A conjunct (non-scalic) contour	3-4
A disjunct contour	6

Pages 10-11: Exercise 2 – Special melodic notes

Position (bar/beat)	Note name	Description
1²	C	Unaccented passing note
1³	A	Lower auxiliary
4¹	A	Appoggiatura
4²	F	Accented passing note
5¹	C♯	Chromatic accented passing note

6¹	A	Lower auxiliary
7¹	F♯	Chromatic lower auxiliary
11³	D	Echappée
12¹	A	Unaccented passing note
12³	B♭	Note of anticipation

Page 11: Exercise 3 – Intervals

Bar	Notes	Interval
2	D – G	Perfect 4th
3	D – B♭	Minor 6th
3-4	F – A	Major 3rd
11	E♭ – C	Minor 3rd
11	F – E♭	Minor 7th
13	E♭ – A	Diminished 5th

Pages 12-14: Exercise 4 – Melodic devices

1. Two balanced 5-bar phrases
2. Motif
3. A lower chromatic auxiliary note
4. Intervallic augmentation
5. Rising sequence
6. Intervallic diminution and inversion
7. Fragmentation
8. Arpeggio
9. Falling by a 3rd
10. Repetition

Pages 14-15: Exercise 5 – Ornamentation

Ornament symbol	Ornament name	How played
A	Acciaccatura	E
B	Appoggiatura	D
C	Trill	B
D	Inverted Mordent	C
E	Mordent	F
F	Turn	A

Page 16: Exercise 6 – Diatonic chords and inversions

I   IV   ii   V   V7d   Ib   vi   ii   iib   iii

vi   iib   ii   Ic   V   Ib   IV   ii7b   Ic   V7   I

Pages 16-18: Exercise 7 – Cadences

Bar	Key	Chords	Cadence
2	G major	IV – I	Plagal
4	G major	Ic – V	Imperfect: half close
6	A minor	ic – V^7 – i	Perfect
8	G major	Ic – V^7 – I	Perfect
10	E minor	ii – V	Imperfect
12	E minor	ivb – V	Imperfect: Phrygian
14	G major	iib – V	Imperfect
16	B minor	i – V	Imperfect
18	G major	iib – V^7 – vi	Interrupted
20	G major	V – I	Perfect (NB 4-3 suspension on V)

Pages 18-20: Exercise 8 – Advanced chords

Chord	Chord analysis
Bar 3^2	Augmented 6th (French)
Bar 5^1	Diminished 7th
Bar 5^2	Secondary dominant 7th (V^7b of IV)
Bar 7^2	Secondary dominant 7th (V^7 of V)
Bar 9^2	Secondary dominant 7th (V^7 of III)
Bar 11	Minor chord iv in C major

Bar 13^2	Augmented 6th (initially Italian, then German)
Bar 18	Neapolitan 6th
Bar 19^1	Diminished 7th
Bar 22	Chord I (Tierce de Picardie)

Page 20: Exercise 9 – Keys: signatures and relationships

1. 5
2. 4
3. C minor
4. A major
5. C minor
6. E major
7. B♭ minor
8. E minor
9. E♭ minor
10. E♭ major

Pages 20-21: Texture words

Texture term	Definition
Monophonic	One instrument or voice playing a single melodic line
Unison	Two or more instruments or voices playing the same melodic line at the same octave
Octaves texture	Two or more instruments or voices playing the same melodic line at two or more different octaves
Parallel 3rds	The same melodic line doubled at the interval of a 3rd
Melody and accompaniment	A distinct melodic line supported by a non-melodic accompaniment

Homophonic	Chordal music
Polyphonic	Two or more different melodic lines heard together (usually in choral music)
Contrapuntal	Two or more different melodic lines heard together (usually in instrumental music)
Fugal	Polyphonic or contrapuntal music which is based on a main melodic theme (the subject) which is heard alternately through each voice
Canonic	Polyphonic or contrapuntal music in which once voice has the same melodic line as another but starting later, and possibly from a different pitch
Antiphonal	Alternation in the texture between two groups of players / singers or registers

Pages 23-25: Question 1

1. Octave
2. Octaves texture
3. Minor
4. Circle of 5ths harmony
5. Bassoon
6. b
7. Relative major (B♭ major)
8. Subdominant (C minor)
9. 3 bars
10. Tonic pedal note
11. Relative of the subdominant
12. c

Pages 26-28: Question 2

1. Bass
2. $\frac{3}{4}$
3. Adagio
4. Dominant
5. Triadic
6. Minor 7th
7. Ic – V⁷ – I
8. Homophony
9. Secondary 7th
10. 5 and 11
11. c
12. d

Pages 31-36: Sample question 25

1. Augmented 4th [1 mark]
2. Circle of 5ths [1 mark]
3. E minor and B minor [2 marks]
4. ii⁷b *or* half diminished 7th on C♯/E [2 marks]
5. Any beat between bar 44^3 and 45^2 [1 mark]
6. Answers should discuss contrasts of:
   - Scoring (tutti sections v. solo passages with basso continuo)
   - Melodic material (ritornello v. solo figurations)
   - Texture (monophonic, octaves, melody and accompaniment, parallel 3rds)
   - Tonality

   ...and give precise locations for examples that support the argument. [10 marks]

[Total: 17 marks]

Pages 37-42: Sample question 26

1. bar 8[3]: it is the 7th in the chord of V^7d

   Bar 9[1]: it is a bass suspension [2 marks]

2. Conjunct [1 mark]

3. Diminished 5th [1 mark]

4. Tonic pedal [2 marks]

5. Antiphonal [1 mark]

6. The music begins in G major with a '1st subject' for Figaro which has an assertive character with simple marching rhythm using repeating crotchets and confident leaps in the contour.

   Whilst still in G major, Susanna enters with a contrasting melodic idea of graceful conjunct quavers, several of which act as appoggiaturas and often slurred pairs of notes to one syllable. The initial direction of the contour is downward. Figaro continues with his leaping interjections. Eventually this passage works as a transition, moving the music to the dominant key.

   The '2nd subject' is then heard at bar 33 in D major. Significantly it takes the form of Figaro singing Susanna's tune: she has captured her fiancé's attention. The music in bar 38-42 acts as a codetta with repeated perfect cadences in the dominant. [10 marks]

[Total: 17 marks]

AoS2: Pop music

Page 48: Harmonic analysis

$D^7/F\sharp$ G C^7 $C\sharp_{dim}$ D^{sus4}

Page 52: Track 1 – Muse, 'Plug in Baby'

1. Electric Guitar [1 mark]

2. 1 chord every 2 bars [1 mark]

3. Perfect [1] 4th [1] [2 marks] [no marks for just perfect]

4. 135bpm [1 mark]

Page 53: Track 2 – Joni Mitchell, 'Both Sides Now' (2000 version)

1. $\frac{4}{4}$, accept common time [1 mark] [no marks for $\frac{2}{4}$]
2. 3rd [1 mark]
3. c [1 mark]
4. Major [1 mark]
5. Suspension [1 mark]

Page 54: Track 3 – Daft Punk, 'Get Lucky'

1. d [1 mark]
2. 2 and 4 [2 marks] [1 mark for each]
3. 7th (C♯ – B) [1 mark]
4. Conjunct [1 mark]

Pages 55-58: Essay question (Section C)

Piece 1: Stevie Wonder 'Superstition' (1972)

Piece 2: Stevie Wonder 'I just called to say I love you' (1984) [1]

Funk as a genre of music emerged in 1960s America [2]*, itself a combination of musical styles. The key characteristics of funk include a complex groove, interjections from the horn section and interlocking drum patterns. 'Superstition' has many of these characteristics, with an opening riff which is now iconic. It uses the Eb minor pentatonic scale with four straight quavers followed by a more complex second part of the bar. The second clavinet* [3] *part plays an Eb major 7 chord underneath this 2-bar riff, giving an Eb*[b7#9] *chord with the major and minor third played simultaneously* [4]*. The bass guitar anchors the riff, playing on the beat Ebs before increased quaver movement in the final two beats of the bar. Wonder's vocals also employ the Ebm pentatonic scale with subtle syncopation over this accompaniment, dovetailing with the three-layered texture.*

The piece develops in three main ways. Firstly, Wonder introduces a horn riff (tenor saxophone and trumpet) at 'thirteen month old baby' [5]*. This new riff has an ascending profile using semiquavers, again employing the pentatonic scale, peaking on a top Bb. The use of ties aids the syncopation. A second development occurs in the short*

---

[1] This list approach quickly outlines the artist and the pieces to be discussed.

[2] A little bit of contextual history is good, but not if it is at the expense of musical detail and takes you away from answering the question.

[3] What does the first clavinet do?

[4] Is this new? Or old? Link to blues/jazz?

[5] Direct reference to the piece - specific

chorus, where the harmonic rhythm changes to two chords per bar, outlining V7, bvi7 and V7 secondary dominant (V7b of V) in minims before settling on IV7 for a whole bar, eventually resolving to a crotchet V+ augmented triad on Bb [6]. This chromatic chord allows for a one bar breakdown to interrupt the flow of the music [7]. Finally, a 4-bar link with the horn section prominently using C natural [8] in a contrasting descending pattern leads into the bridge which repeats the chorus chords complete with a vocal 'howl'.

In a similar way to how funk as a musical style developed from a combination of older musical styles, R&B also went through a similar transformation. Whilst the style could be argued to have started in 1940s America, by the 1980s a more contemporary R&B sound world had developed which combines elements of funk, dance, rhythm and blues and hip hop. 'I just called to say I love you' is a contrasting piece by Wonder which shows this change in musical genre [9].

The piece has a more relaxed [10] nature when compared to 'Superstition' owing to the lush string synths and lack of rhythmic groove or horn section, using subtle melodic syncopation in the vocal line. An opening sustained Db major chord with bass alternating between tonic and dominant every two beats acts as a 4-bar introduction before the verse starts with a simple melody outlining dominant – tonic via the leading note, giving a yearning quality [11]. The drum beat is programmed using a drum machine and the entire piece has an iconic 1980s sound. In a similar way to 'Superstition', the vocal lines use short phrases with an ascending profile, but rather than being pentatonic in construction the melody has a wider compass. Harmonically, the verse is rooted in the tonic Db with a chord sequence which also includes the dominant Ab and the secondary dominant Ebm. The harmonic rhythm is slow in the verses, with chords usually being settled on for several bars at a time.

In contrast, the chorus moves to a faster harmonic rhythm [12] with one chord per bar (Ebm – Ab – Db – Db). On the second line of the chorus, a Bbm chord is introduced (the relative minor – 'care') replacing the tonic chord and giving an interrupted cadence. Wonder then

[6] Mention use of sextuplet as a new rhythmic idea in combination with this chromatic chord?

[7] This could be expanded

[8] Why is this so important given the music heard up to this point?

[9] At 82 words, this is a lengthy way of giving context and potentially distracts from the musical detail required for a top answer.

[10] Musical term?

[11] Achieved, in part, by the leading note also having the longest rhythmic value (dotted crotchet)

[12] Comparison to 'Superstition'?

repeats the chorus, moving up a semitone to D major, then again to Eb major, before an instrumental section which repeats the entire process using vocalise in the lyrics, giving a computerised sound effect. For the final repetition in Eb major, Wonder's melody competes with the vocalise which now act as backing vocals in the gaps of the main melody. A short coda using a 2-bar sequence initiates a harmonic change, using Cb major and Db major (sus2) chords which then resolve back to the (new) tonic Eb major.

Both of these pieces demonstrate how one artist can encompass different musical styles throughout a career, as well as showing how musical genres achieve contrast by development of the styles which have come before them [13].

[13] The conclusion does draw the argument to a close, is short, and links to the style of music referenced in the question.

Comment: The essay contains lots of interesting analysis and fully answers the question. There is a little too much description of context, and some opportunities to contrast the pieces are missed. Nevertheless, this is confident writing with a convincing essay style.

AoS3: Music for media

Pages 60-61: Harmonic analysis

I+   vi   V   V7d   Ib   IV   V7   I

Page 61: Complex chords

Given the nature of this AoS you should be able to find many examples of these chords.

Chord	Symbol	Notation	Example
Augmented triad C – E – G♯	C⁺		Herrmann – *Psycho 'Prelude'*
Added 6th chord	C⁶		
Diminished triad	C°		
Diminished 7th	C⁷°		
Half diminished 7th	Cø		

Pages 64-65: Track 1 – Hans Zimmer, *The Lion King* 'King of Pride Rock'

1. (Violon)cello [1 mark]
2. $\frac{3}{4}$ [1 mark]
3. b [1 mark]
4. Semiquaver [1 mark]
5. Submediant [1 mark]

Page 65: Track 2 – Nobuo Uematsu, *Lost Odyssey* '103 The Gun Barrel Battle'

1. Minor [1 mark]
2. Trill [1 mark]
3. c [1 mark]
4. Brass [1 mark]
5. 9-8 suspension [1 mark]

ANSWERS

Page 66: Track 3 – Bernard Herrmann, *North by Northwest* 'The Crash'

Award marks according to the following band descriptions:

9-10	A comprehensive and authoritative response which is consistently coherent and logically structured
7-8	A wide-ranging and confident response which is mostly coherent and well structured
5-6	A relevant response despite some inaccuracy/ omission and weaknesses in terms of coherency and structure
3-4	A limited response with some significant inaccuracy/ omission and a lack of clarity
1-2	A rudimentary response
0	No work submitted or worthy of credit.

Reference could be made to:

Flying: fast tempo, loud dynamics, ascending patterns, glissando, mechanical sounding motor rhythms in strings taken up by tambourine, syncopation, minor key, fragmented melodic lines (bar by bar approach), dissonance within a minor temperature

Crash: use of cymbals/percussion, use of semiquavers, fast tempo, crescendo, dissonance, fade out at end of scene

Any other valid points.

Pages 66-71: Essay question (Section C)

Comment on Candidate A:

This essay is heavy on non-musical description with the entire first paragraph – nearly a third of the essay – having no musical detail whatsoever.

When the musical analysis does start there is some acknowledgement of relevant issues, with D minor and the opening theme correctly identified. However, description soon comes again to the fore as the plot is described at the expense of musical detail. There are inaccuracies too – the male vocal line (F-E-F-G♯) is more than just semitones and the comment 'trills and crescendos add interest' does not qualify what is being made more interesting. G major is not the relative major of D minor. The language is colloquial and short on perceptive musical comment. The candidate also incorrectly suggests Herrmann as the named artist – it is of course Zimmer. The second piece is correctly identified as being in ternary form – though the title of the piece is not given. The main tune is again identified, though no link is made to the idea of leitmotif. The conclusion is short on style and highlights the fact that the candidate has not addressed the requirements of the question. The essay is short for 45 minutes.

Comment on Candidate B:

The introduction moves directly into addressing the question and using correct musical vocabulary, introducing both pieces. There is a clear essay style from the outset.

The musical analysis shows a commanding grasp of relevant issues and assured musical understanding, with the aural experience being clear throughout. There is a high level of music analysis and description is mostly avoided in a mature writing style. The plot is not described without appropriate analytical detail. There is little mention of textural changes in either piece, though harmonic and melodic detail is often strong. The conclusion is stylish, addressing the question.

AoS4: Music for theatre

Page 76: Study Piece 2: Schönberg, *Les Miserables* 'Empty Chairs at Empty Tables'

1st playing	■ Sonority – male tenor (a cappella), strings accompaniment, plucked broken chord ■ Minor key – A minor ■ $\frac{4}{4}$, moderato ■ Song form – A sections repeat, key change at the end
2nd playing	■ Conjunct, often falling – grief. Some disjunct moments 'I can hear' compound 2nd ■ Accompaniment figure – rising broken chord with 9th ■ Some suspensions (upward resolving 9ths), 7ths ■ Tertiary modulation to C♯m towards end
3rd playing	■ Slow in A sections faster in B section – structure link ■ Regular phrases, repetition ■ Melody and accompaniment, drops out at 'lonely barricade' (word painting), a cappella at start ■ Revolutionary France (early 19th century), late 20th century musical – epic
4th playing	■ Confirm the 32-bar song form ■ Add in countermelody between vocal breaks – cor anglais? ■ Any other valid points

Page 77: Track 1 – Claude-Michel Schönberg, *Miss Saigon* 'I still believe'

1. Minor 2nd (A-B♭) [2 marks] [Award 1 mark for '2nd']
2. Minor [1 mark]
3. c [1 mark]
4. Circle of Fifths [1 mark]

Page 78: Track 2 – Richard Rodgers, *Oklahoma!* 'I cain't say no'

1. Moderato [1 mark]
2. b (fix – up to a C, nix – down to an F) [1 mark]
3. Ostinato [1 mark]
4. Melody and Accompaniment [1 mark]
5. Octave [1 mark]

Page 79: Track 3 – Stephen Sondheim, *Sweeney Todd* 'Opening Ballad'

Award marks according to the following band descriptions:

9-10	A comprehensive and authoritative response which is consistently coherent and logically structured
7-8	A wide-ranging and confident response which is mostly coherent and well structured
5-6	A relevant response despite some inaccuracy/omission and weaknesses in terms of coherency and structure
3-4	A limited response with some significant inaccuracy/omission and a lack of clarity
1-2	A rudimentary response
0	No work submitted or worthy of credit.

Reference could be made to:

Opening section:

Minor key, pedal point, $\frac{6}{8}$ compound time, quavers G♯/A, use of flattened 7th – modal character, subtle dynamic changes, use of dissonant whistle, ostinato shapes, solo voice (2 characters)

Second section:

Chorus enters – 3 parts (STB), Dies Irae motif, homophony, subito fortissimo, E♯ (leading note) used but does not resolve to tonic, dissonant chords, chromaticism in tenor, return to opening quavers at end.

Any other valid points.

Pages 79-82: Essay question (Section C)

The essay content is covered in the chapter and within Study Piece 2 above. Like all essays it should be marked to the assessment grid within the specification on the AQA website, here: http://filestore.aqa.org.uk/resources/music/AQA-72711-SMS.PDF

AoS5: Jazz

Page 85: Blues scales

Hexatonic Scale:

Heptatonic Scale:

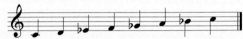

Nonotonic Scale:

Pages 88-89: Track 1 – Louis Armstrong, 'West End Blues'

1. Trumpet [1 mark]
2. Crotchets [1 mark]
3. a [1 mark]
4. Chalumeau [1 mark]
5. Glissando [1 mark, accept slide, do not accept portamento]

Page 89: Track 2 – Duke Ellington, 'Black and Tan Fantasy'

1. Pitch-bend [1 mark]
2. Syncopation [1 mark]
3. Mute [1 mark]
4. Alto Saxophone [1 mark]
5. Descending sequence [1 mark]

Page 90: Track 3 – Miles Davis, 'All Blues'

1. 3rds [1 mark]
2. $\frac{6}{4}$ [1 mark]
3. 6th [1 mark]
4. Brushes [1 mark]
5. Modal [1 mark]

Page 90: Track 4 – Charlie Parker, 'A Night in Tunisia'

Award marks according to the following band descriptions:

9-10	A comprehensive and authoritative response which is consistently coherent and logically structured
7-8	A wide-ranging and confident response which is mostly coherent and well structured
5-6	A relevant response despite some inaccuracy/ omission and weaknesses in terms of coherency and structure
3-4	A limited response with some significant inaccuracy/ omission and a lack of clarity
1-2	A rudimentary response
0	No work submitted or worthy of credit.

Reference could be made to:

Instrumental virtuosity – alto sax and trumpet, using fast scalic passages. Piano/guitar/bass riff.

Tempo and rhythm – fast tempo, swung rhythms

Melody – melodic lines are reliant on chord extensions, making them complex. Wide ranging intervals. Riff uses rising arpeggio idea, omitting the third and containing flattened 7th in the first bar and having a complete triad plus a 6th in the second bar, alternating between E♭ and D giving a Phrygian modal character.

Harmony – D minor with blue notes and extensive chromaticism. V[7] used, as is Neapolitan as a tritone substitution for V[7].

Any other valid points.

Pages 91-92: Essay question (Section C)

The Miles Davis work has some relevant information and is particularly strong on harmonic analysis. However, only the first few bars are really discussed, and while the harmonic analysis is correct it is a little descriptive in nature. There is little discussion on the melodic features of the music. Some attempt is made to explain the bebop style, but this is again brief and prone to description.

To improve it, rewrite this paragraph to include more perceptive analysis, greater musical detail and further examples to help justify your response. Consider which piece you could use as a contrast, ensuring you use comparative language to address the question.

AoS6: Contemporary traditional music

Pages 94-95: String techniques

Name	Evidence	Description
Chicharra	http://bit.ly/ Chicharra	'cricket' – using the heel of the bow to play on the cotton part of the D string of the violin to create a percussive, low pitch squeak
Latigo	http://bit.ly/ TangoLatigo	'whip' – played on the E string of the violin using a slow to fast bow coupled with a glissando up or down the string
Arrastre	http://bit.ly/ Arrastre	'to drag' – slow to fast bow acceleration into a downbeat; often used in the bass part
Tambor	http://bit.ly/ TangoTambor	'small drum' – placement of second finger against the G but finger on the D with accented pizzicato on the G string giving a percussive, dry sound
Golpe de Caja	http://bit.ly/ GalopeDeCaja	'hit the box' – striking the box of the string instrument using a hand, fingers, with or without rings, to create different percussive sounds

Pages 97-98: Track 1 – Anoushka Shankar and Norah Jones, 'Unsaid'

1. Sitar [1 mark]
2. Moderato [1 mark]
3. d [1 mark]
4. Pitch Bend [1 mark]
5. c [1 mark]

Pages 98-99: Track 2 – Diabaté, 'Solo'

1. Kora [1 mark]
2. Major 3rd (C-E) [1 mark]
3. Swung rhythms [1 mark]
4. Descending, Syncopation [2 marks]

Page 99: Track 3 – Bellowhead, 'London Town'

1. Accordion [1 mark]
2. Syncopated [1 mark]
3. a [1 mark]
4. 2 and 4 [2 marks]

Page 100: Track 4 – Piazzolla, 'Knife Fight'

Agitated – dissonant tremolo forte chords on piano, use of latigo (whip) on violin, dissonant accordion chords, syncopation, accented motor rhythms, minor thirds ascent/descent in bass, modulation to subdominant, stab chords.

Climax – increased rhythmic drive to the climax of the piece – bass semiquavers. Descending profile to melodic ideas.

Ending – latigo violin, descending profile, dissonant chords, diminuendo, reduced rhythmic drive, victim falling to floor – high-low glissando on violin (siren?), three final stabs of the dissonant chord.

Page 100: Essay question (Section C)

Mark your essay to the assessment grid within the specification on the AQA website, here: http://filestore.aqa.org.uk/resources/music/AQA-72711-SMS.PDF

Glossary

12-bar blues One of the most prominent chord progressions in popular music, starting in blues music and spreading to jazz, rock, R&B, etc.

32-bar song form A name sometimes used for **popular song form** when each phrase is eight bars long.

A cappella Unaccompanied singing; from the Italian meaning 'in the chapel style', this term originally applied to church music, but is now used in contemporary vocal music.

Acciaccatura An ornament printed as a small note with a slash through its tail, which is played as quickly as possible before the main note that follows it; also known as a grace note.

Additive rhythm A rhythm where the bar is divided into beats of unequal length, e.g. 3+3+2.

Alap The opening section of a piece of Indian classical music, usually with melodic improvisation and free rhythm, developing into a **raga**.

Anacrusis One or more weak-beat notes before the first strong beat of a phrase, which is often called a 'pick up' in pop music (plural: anacruses).

Antecedent and consequent phrases Used to describe a pairing of phrases, typically found in **periodic phrasing**. Alternatively, the second phrase may be called an answering phrase. The two phrases will match in length, usually in rhythm, and sometimes in contour.

Antiphony, antiphonal A musical texture where two groups of musicians take it in turns to play; can also refer to sections of alternating registers.

Appoggiatura A melodic ornament where a neighbouring note (that sounds dissonant) is sounded for a measured period of time before the main note of the melody. In the Romantic era appoggiaturas are also found in the accompanying harmonic texture.

Arco An instruction for string players to use the bow, after playing pizzicato.

Aria An extended vocal solo in an opera, oratorio or cantata.

Arpeggio The notes of a standard triad played one after another, in ascending or descending order, that is, the 1st, 3rd, 5th and 8th notes of a scale.

Arrastre From Spanish, meaning 'drag', a specialist bow stroke that changes the bow speed from slow to fast, usually onto the downbeat. Often heard in the double bass part of an **orquesta típica**.

Articulation How smoothly or otherwise the notes are played, e.g. very detached (**staccato**), or joined together (**legato**) are types of articulation.

Atonal, atonality Western music without an obvious home key. Atonal music avoids major and minor keys (and also **modes**).

Augmentation Literally means 'expanded'. The opposite of **diminution**. It can refer to various features:

- **Interval**: an augmented interval is a semitone wider than a major or perfect interval, e.g. C-D♯, C-F♯
- **Chord**: a triad made up of two major 3rds, e.g. C-E-G♯

- **Rhythm**: a proportionate increase in the note lengths of a melody, for example, when two quavers and a crotchet are augmented they become two crotchets and a minim.

Auxiliary note A melodic decoration and non-harmony note one step away from the chord onto which it resolves, creating **dissonance.** They can be higher or lower than the chord, and so described as upper or lower auxiliary notes respectively. Where an accidental is used to create an auxiliary note that is a semitone away from the harmony note, this is called a **chromatic auxiliary note**.

Backbeat A term used in pop music to describe accenting the normally weak second and fourth beats in $\frac{4}{4}$ time.

Bare 5ths A texture where a melodic line is simultaneously played (doubled) a 5th higher or lower, thus creating a sparse, hollow effect, sometimes reminiscent of medieval organum (a style associated with monastic singing): see also open 5ths.

Basso continuo The fundamental basis of most orchestral and ensemble music in the Baroque period, represented in the score by the bass line that includes **figured bass** notation. This is played by a bass instrument (typically a cello, possibly a bassoon or other options) and a harmony instrument (harpsichord, organ or lute).

Bebop A style of jazz developed in the 1940s, notable for fast tempos, complex harmonies, virtuosic playing and much use of improvisation.

Belt A style of singing sometimes found in music theatre and pop music in which the singer uses their chest voice (usually a low register sound) above its natural range with a very loud dynamic.

Binary form A musical structure of two sections each of which is repeated to give ‖: A :‖: B :‖. The A section usually modulates to the dominant (or relative major); the B section starts in the dominant (or relative major) and returns to the tonic. Sometimes the B section refers to the opening tune of the A section to mark the return to the tonic key; this is known as **rounded binary form**.

Birimintingo Improvised solo melodic runs in kora playing.

Blue note In blues music, notes used in the melodic line which do not belong to the fundamental major key of the music, e.g. a flattened 3rd or flattened 7th.

Break A short instrumental solo, often improvised, in pop and jazz.

Breakdown A section of a song where various instrumentalists all have solo **breaks**.

Bridge A contrasting section in a pop song which usually joins the verse to the chorus, or is heard after twice through the verse and chorus.

Broken chord A chord in which the notes are sounded individually, or spread, rather than all being played exactly together. An arpeggio is a type of broken chord.

Cadence A pair of chords which mark the end of a musical statement. See p16 for perfect, imperfect, plagal and interrupted cadences.
- **Half-close** A type of imperfect cadence, Ic-V
- **Phrygian** ivb-V in a minor key, where the bass line moves down a semitone and the top line moves

up a tone; common in Baroque music, and another type of imperfect cadence

- **Cadential 6/4** A second inversion chord resolving to the dominant, so Ic-V, another type of imperfect cadence

Call and response Vocal music in which a soloist sings a phrase to which a group of singers respond. Found in African music, as well as in jazz and pop music.

Canon A contrapuntal device in which a melody in one part is repeated note for note in another part starting a few beats later (and possibly at a different pitch), while the melody in the first part continues to unfold.

Chalumeau register The lowest range of a clarinet, with a rich, dark tone.

Chicharra In tango music, a technique where the violinist plays the strings *behind* the bridge, with heavy downward pressure on the bow, to emulate the sound of a cicada or cricket.

Chorus In music technology, when two sounds with similar timbral qualities are placed together to sound as one.

Chromatic Notes that don't belong to the current key; the opposite of **diatonic.**

Circle of 5ths progression A series of chords whose roots are each a perfect 5th lower than the previous chord.

Cluster chord A chord of at least three adjacent notes (probably semitones).

Coda The final section of a composition; where following repeated sections, such as in **32-bar song form**, the coda will be different from earlier sections.

Codetta A coda to a section of music, e.g. in sonata form, the close of an exposition section before the development starts.

Colla voce Literally meaning 'with the voice', indicating a freer tempo for the soloist, and the accompanying instruments should follow.

Col legno Played with the wood of a bow, rather than the hair, producing a dry sound.

Compound interval Intervals which are greater than an octave, so compound 5th describes an octave (or even two octaves) plus a 5th.

Compound time A metre in which the main beat can be subdivided into three. Common time signatures are $\frac{6}{8}$, $\frac{12}{8}$, $\frac{6}{4}$. The opposite of **Simple time**.

Conjunct A style of melodic writing in which each note is a step away from the previous one.

Consonant (harmony) A combination of notes providing a pleasing sound when played together, the opposite of **dissonant**. This is generally achieved by avoiding notes that are a semitone, tone or tritone apart.

Con sordino Played with a mute on the instrument thereby altering the timbre (on bowed string instruments and brass instruments).

Contour As contours on a map indicate the ups and downs of a landscape, this term is used to describe the rise and fall (or shape) of a melody line, such as ascending, descending, scalic, arpeggio, conjunct, disjunct.

Contrapuntal Music that uses **counterpoint**, a texture where two or more melodic lines are played together at the same time.

Cool jazz A lighter style of jazz, with a laid-back style of relaxed tempos, contrasting with the earlier **bebop** style.

Countermelody An independent melody sounding against another melody which has already been heard.

Counterpoint The simultaneous combination of two or more melodies with independent rhythms. There may be some imitation between parts, but counterpoint can also be non-imitative. A whole movement may be contrapuntal, or the music may alternate between contrapuntal and other textures. This term is often used interchangeably with **polyphony,** but is more commonly used for instrumental music.

Cross-rhythm A pattern in which the rhythmic detail of the music is out of phase with the underlying pulse (as in a **hemiola**), or where different subdivisions of the beat are used simultaneously (as in duple and triplet quavers).

Delay Guitar device which records a sound and repeats it at a given time, or multiple times, often with a diminuendo. Not to be confused with an echo, which does not repeat the sound.

Diatonic Music using just the notes of the home key; the opposite of **chromatic**.

Diegetic music Music that is heard in a film, the source of which is part of the film, such as the band in the saloon, the busker on the street, the organ in the church.

Diminished chord A triad made up of two minor 3rds, e.g. C-E♭-G♭. A diminished 7th is made up of three minor 3rds.

Diminution Literally means 'reduced'. The opposite of **augmentation**. It can refer to various features:

- **Interval**: a diminished interval is a semitone narrower than a major or perfect interval, e.g. C-D♭, C-G♭
- **Chord**: a triad made up of two minor 3rds, e.g. C-E♭-G♭
- **Rhythm**: a proportionate reduction in the note lengths of a melody, for example, when two quavers and a crotchet are diminished they become two semiquavers and a quaver.

Disjunct A style of melodic writing including many leaps between one note and the next; opposite of **conjunct**.

Dissonant, dissonance A combination of notes producing a clashing sound when played together; opposite of **consonant.**

Distortion A technological effect used to alter the sound of an amplified instrument, usually creating a 'dirty' or 'clipped' version of the same sound.

Dominant 7th Literally the note that is a 7th above the dominant; however, it is usually used to describe the dominant chord when the 7th note is included. The result is very direction-inducing, usually requiring resolution onto the tonic chord.

Doubled, doubling More than one part playing the same line, either in unison or an octave apart. Doubling of a melody can also occur at other intervals, e.g. at a 3rd for a consonant effect, or at a 4th for a more spikey, aggressive effect.

Double stopping Two notes played at the same time on a stringed instrument on two adjacent strings.

Double time In jazz, an instruction to change to using notes of double speed (e.g. semiquavers instead of quavers) without changing the underlying tempo of the chord progression. Often used in improvised solos.

Drone One or more notes held or repeated throughout an extended passage of music. Some instruments, such as bagpipes and sitar, have an inbuilt drone.

Echappée note An unaccented, dissonant melodic decoration note, that is one step higher or lower than the essential note, and then resolves by a leap back to the harmony note.

Enharmonic Two notes or keys which sound the same but are written differently, such as C♯ and D♭.

Episode A solo passage occurring in a **ritornello** movement.

Extended chord A triad with notes added to it, such as a 7th, 9th, 11th or 13th.

Fado Portuguese traditional sung ballad.

False relation A simultaneous or adjacent occurrence in different parts of a note in its natural form and its sharpened or flattened form.

Fill In pop music, a mini instrumental solo between the phrases of a song; the term is usually used with the name of the instrument playing, e.g. drum fill.

Four-on-the-floor Bass drum of a drum kit, playing on every crotchet in a $\frac{4}{4}$ bar, common in disco music of the 1970s.

Fours In jazz, when the players in the band take turns performing solos or improvisations for four bars. Usually this keeps going back to the drummer, for instance in a piano trio: Piano > Drums > Bass > Drums > Piano, etc.

Foursquare A passage of four 4-bar phrases. It is a less sophisticated version of **periodic phrasing** where there is a clear hierarchy of 2-bar, 4-bar and 8-bar pairings.

Fragmentation A compositional technique of breaking down a theme into its constituent motifs and repeating and developing them.

French 6th An augmented chord containing the root, major 3rd, augmented 4th and augmented 6th.

Fugue, fugal A contrapuntal musical form in which a main theme is taken up and developed by each part in turn.

Functional harmony A term sometimes used to describe standard tonal harmony in which primary and secondary triads are used with a sense of hierarchy and direction, and chromatic inflexions are understood in terms of conventions such as **secondary dominant 7ths**.

German 6th An augmented 6th chord containing the root, major 3rd, perfect 5th and augmented 6th.

Ghost note In jazz, a note with a rhythmic value but no obvious pitch, notated with an 'x' in place of a note head.

Glissando A compositional technique requiring the pitch to slide from one note to another: see also **portamento**.

Golpe de Caja From Spanish, meaning 'hit on the box'. In tango, an instruction to string players to hit the box part of the instrument. This can be done in a variety of ways, such as thumb knuckles or palm, each creating a different sound. More likely on the double bass, but also possible on the violin.

Groove A jazz term for the rhythmic 'feel' of a piece of music.

Habanera rhythm Traditional dance rhythm of Cuban and South American music.

Hard bop A subgenre of jazz, developed from bebop, with hard, funky rhythms and blues influence.

Harmonic rhythm The rate at which the harmony changes in a piece of music.

Harmonic series On many instruments these are the notes which occur 'naturally', due to the way a string vibrates or the air vibrates in a brass instrument to create certain pitches.

Harmonics On string instruments, including harp and guitar, a very high, pure sound produced by placing a finger on a string very lightly before plucking or bowing.

Harmon mute A **wah-wah mute** for brass instruments.

Hemiola A rhythmic device in which two groups of three beats (*strong-weak-weak, strong-weak-weak*) are performed as three groups of two (*strong-weak, strong-weak, strong-weak*).

Heptatonic A 7-note scale: see p85.

Heterophony, heterophonic Simultaneous performance of a melody and a variation of the melody. In jazz this is often when one player improvises on the melody while another plays it straight.

Hexatonic A 6-note scale: see p85.

Homophony, homophonic A musical texture in which all parts (melody and accompaniment) move in similar rhythm creating a chordal effect.

Hook A repeated, catchy **motif** in jazz and pop music.

Interval The distance between two pitches: count the letter names between the notes including the first and last, so C to G is a 5th. See also **compound interval**.

Inversion (of a chord) A chord is inverted when a note other than the root is in the bass (e.g. chord V). In first inversion the 3rd is in the bass (Vb); in second inversion the 5th is in the bass (Vc). The chord of the dominant 7th can be written in third inversion (V^7d).

Inversion (of a melody) When the intervals in a melody stay the same, but the pitch moves in the opposite direction, e.g. ascends instead of descending. The result is akin to a mirror image of the melodic **contour**.

Inverted pedal See the explanation for **Pedal note**; an inverted pedal note sounds higher than the harmonies beneath it, instead of lower.

Italian 6th An augmented chord containing the root, major 3rd and augmented 6th.

Kumbengo An ostinato pattern in kora playing.

Latigo Spanish for 'whip', a type of glissando in tango music. It is played fast, ascending or descending, to mimic the sound of a whip (as used by Argentine gauchos).

Latin rhythm Music of South America and Cuba is characterised by syncopated rhythms and beats of unequal length, e.g. 3 + 3 + 2.

Legato Played smoothly, without breaks between the notes.

Leitmotif A recurring fragment of music that represents a specific character, event or emotion.

Looping A technique in electroacoustic music and sound production in which a short passage of sound material (the loop) is repeated to create **ostinato** patterns. Loops can be created in many ways, including sampler, synthesiser, sequencer, drum machine, and computer.

Marcato Marked, or accented playing.

Melisma A series of melodic notes sung to the same syllable.

Mickey-mousing A technique in film music of synchronising the accompanying music directly to action on screen. The term is derived from early Walt Disney films.

Middle 8 The central, contrasting section of a song, in pop and jazz music, also called the bridge, or B section in an AABA song form. Often, but not always, 8 bars long.

Milonga A type of tango dance.

Mixolydian Major scale with a flattened 7th.

Mode, modal, modality An alternative series of scales to the diatonic major and minor scales, often used in traditional music.

Modulation The process of changing key midway through a piece.

Monophony, monophonic Music consisting of a single unaccompanied melody line.

Mordent A melodic ornament.

Motif, motivic A short, distinctive musical idea: see also **leitmotif**.

Motor rhythm An insistently repeating short rhythmic pattern that conveys an almost mechanical, unstoppable quality, a typical example being two semiquavers plus a quaver.

Mute Device attached to an instrument to soften the tone and produce a different timbre, for string and brass instruments; see **con sordino.**

Neapolitan chord Major chord based on the lowered supertonic (second note) of the scale. Most commonly it appears in a minor key and in first inversion, when it becomes a **Neapolitan 6th**, so in the key of E minor, this is a chord of F major in first inversion. Romantic period composers first began to use it in root position, then preface it with its own **secondary dominant 7th**, and then explore using it in a major key. The chord usually resolves to the dominant.

Neapolitan key The key found a semitone higher than the tonic key.

Nonatonic A 9-note scale: see p85.

Non-functional harmony Harmony where the chord progressions do not follow the needs (functions) of standard harmony: **see functional harmony**. In non-functional harmony chords are used for their inherent 'colour' rather than for their customary progressive function.

Non-harmony note A note outside of the harmony with which it is sounding, so usually dissonant.

Note of anticipation A non-harmony note which is approached by step from the note before, and then stays the same as the harmony changes for the following melodic note: essentially it is a note from the next chord played early.

Nuevo tango Modern style of tango music, introducing new instruments such as saxophone and electric guitar; strongly associated with Astor Piazzolla.

Octatonic An 8-note scale: see p86.

Open-5th chord A chord containing only the root and 5th, with the 3rd missing. See also **bare 5ths** and **power chord**.

Ostinato A rhythmic, melodic or harmonic pattern repeated many times in succession (similar to a riff in pop music).

Panning In music technology, altering the left and right distribution of the sound.

Parallel 3rds A texture where a melodic line is simultaneously played (doubled) a 3rd higher or lower, thus creating a consonant richness.

Parallel harmony The parallel movement of two or more lines often producing chords with an identical intervallic structure.

Passing note A non-harmony note placed between and connecting two harmony notes, each of which are usually a 3rd apart. Passing notes are usually unaccented (on the half beat, or second and fourth quarter beats), but can be accented (on the beat, with no accent symbol required).

Pedal note A sustained or regularly repeated note, usually heard in the bass, while the harmony above changes between various chords. Usually the pedal note is the tonic or dominant.

Pentatonic scale A scale of only five notes. The most well-known is formed by the black notes of the piano (C♯, E♭, F♯, G♯, B♭) and is anhemitonic, meaning that there are no semitones included (only tones and minor 3rds); alternatively, the pentatonic scale of C, E, F, G, B is hemitonic, as it has a semitone between E and F.

Periodic phrasing Music, typically of the Classical period, in which the melodic phrase is structured in pairs of 2-bar mini-phrases making pairs of 4-bar phrases, making pairs of longer 8-bar phrases, and then 16-bar phrases, and so on.

Phrygian mode Minor key with a flattened second note, a scale with a dark character.

Pitch-bend A short slide up or down to the main note.

Pizzicato An instruction for string players to pluck the string instead of using the bow.

Polarised Texture common in Baroque music where high-pitched instruments are accompanied by a bass continuo, without instruments included in the middle range. More recently, polarised texture is often used in film music as it portrays an expansiveness (e.g. for a landscape scene) and allows dialogue to be clearly heard spoken in mid-register.

Polyphony, polyphonic A musical texture where two or more parts move independently of one another.

Popular song form A common structure in songs in music theatre and popular music, in which there are four phrases where the first, second and fourth are related to give a pattern of AABA: see also **32-bar song form**.

Portamento A performing technique of sliding from one pitch to another, often associated with singing: see **glissando**.

Power chord In pop and rock music, a chord that consists of the root and the 5th, especially on electric guitars and often used with distortion: see **open 5th chord**.

Primary triads Chords I, IV and V in any key, so called because they are of a primary importance in establishing the tonality of a composition.

Push rhythm A rhythm that anticipates the beat, often entering a quaver earlier than expected, and sometimes tied to the first note of the bar to heighten the effect.

Raga A scale pattern or melodic motif used as the basis for melodic improvisation in Indian classical music.

Recitative A type of vocal music where the words are the important element, and are usually sung in free time and in normal speech rhythm.

Relative major/minor A pair of keys which share the same key signature, one major and one minor: for example, the relative minor of F major is D minor, and the relative major of D minor is F major.

Resolution The release of tension in music as the harmony moves from a discord to a concord, or point of tonal stability.

Reverb An electronically-produced echo.

Riff In jazz, pop and rock, a short, catchy melodic or rhythmic idea repeated throughout a song.

Rip In jazz, a quick upwards glissando to a note.

Ripieno In Baroque music, this is the ensemble who play the tutti sections, in contrast to the soloists.

Ritenuto Immediately slowing down.

Ritornello The main structural form for concerto movements in the late Baroque era. The term is also used to name the orchestral section heard at the opening and returns in various keys throughout a movement, punctuated by vocal solos (**episodes**). The ritornello may be repeated whole, or in part, or with variations.

Rondo A musical structure popular in the Classical period in which a main melody alternates with a contrasting section (ABACA).

Root position A triad with its fundamental note in the bass line.

Rubato An interpretative performance technique, often associated with Romantic music, where some nuanced flexibility of rhythm is used (both holding back and pushing on) to create expressive affect.

Scale Eight notes, making up all the notes in a key. The degrees of the scale have the following names:
- I   Tonic
- II   Supertonic (i.e. above the tonic)
- IIII Mediant (i.e. halfway to the dominant)
- IV   Subdominant (i.e. the 5th below the tonic)
- V   Dominant (i.e. the most dominant overtone to the tonic)
- VI   Submediant (i.e. halfway to the subdominant when descending)
- VII Leading note (i.e. leading to the tonic)
- VIII Tonic

Secondary dominant 7th A dominant triad which resolves to a chord that is not the tonic, often the dominant of the dominant, V^7 of V.

Secondary triad Chords ii, iii, vi and sometimes vii in any key, i.e. excluding those which are primary chords.

Sequence (in melody) The immediate repetition of a **motif** or phrase in the same instrumental or vocal part but at a different pitch.

Simple time A metre in which the main beat can be subdivided into two. The opposite of **Compound time**.

Simultaneous quodlibet A composition combining several different pre-existing melodies all heard at the same time, often light-hearted in manner.

Smear In jazz, a loud, possibly coarse, slide away from a note.

Sonata form The most common structure for the first movement (and sometimes other movements) of compositions in the Classical style, comprising exposition, development and recapitulation.

Sotto voce Meaning literally 'under the voice', an indication that a hushed or whispered performance is required.

Source music In a film, music which is played on instruments seen in the film, such as a string quartet at a wedding.

Staccato Short, detached playing, with gaps between the notes.

Stop time In jazz, a rhythm where some beats are not played, e.g. 1 2 (rest) 4, 1 2 (rest) 4.

Substitution chord A complex chord which functions in the same way as the simple chord it replaces.

Sul ponticello Direction to a string player to bow very close to the bridge, producing a whistling tone.

Sul tasto Direction to a string player to bow or pluck the strings over the fingerboard, producing a gentler tone.

Sus4 chord Major or minor chord where the 3rd is omitted and replaced with a 4th, creating an open sound without the 3rd and a dissonance between the 4th and 5th.

Suspension A note from a previous chord is carried over to the following chord, creating dissonance, before resolving. There are four categories: three are understood in terms of the interval above the bass (4-3, 7-6, 9-8), and the fourth is where the suspended note is in the bass.

Swing In jazz and blues style, the first quaver of a pair will often be played slightly longer than the second one.

Syllabic Vocal music in which each syllable of the lyrics is sung to a single note: see also **melisma**.

Sympathetic strings Also called resonance strings, these are auxiliary strings on an instrument which vibrate when the main strings are being played, providing a halo of sound around the note that is being played.

Syncopation The effect created when accented notes are sounded off the beat or on weak beats.

Tala Rhythmic patterns used in Indian music.

Tambor In tango, a form of pizzicato that causes the string to rebound off your finger creating an unpitched drum-like sound.

Tenuto From the Italian 'to hold', this direction indicates the player should hold a note slightly longer than written, often for emphasis.

Ternary form A musical structure of three sections with similar outer sections and a contrasting central one (ABA). Usually the B section is in a contrasting key to the A sections. Can also be described as arch form.

Tessitura The average range of an instrumental, or more usually a vocal, piece. It is worthy of remark if a piece is written high or low in the range of the instrument or voice performing it.

Through-composed A song where each verse is set to contrasting music.

Tierce de Picardie A major tonic chord used to end a piece of music in a minor key.

GLOSSARY

Tonal The use of standard major and minor keys. Not all music is tonal: see also **modal** and **atonal**.

Tremolando A musical effect created by the rapid repetition of a single note, usually associated with string instruments.

Triad, triadic A melody based on the notes of the triad: the root, 3rd and 5th above it. A triad can be major, minor, diminished or augmented.

Trill An ornament: a fast oscillation with the note above or below the given note.

Tritone An interval of an augmented 4th (or diminished 5th), so called because an alternative way of counting it is as an interval of three tones. It so happens that this is exactly half an octave.

Tritone substitution Common in jazz, a chord where a dominant 7th chord is replaced by another dominant 7th chord whose root is a tritone away.

Turn A melodic ornament.

Underscore Music that is played under dialogue in a film score.

Unison Two or more people performing the same note or melody; in a choir when everyone is singing the same melody, even though the men are singing an octave lower than the women.

Verse-chorus form Simple song form common in pop music, alternating verses and chorus which contrast with one another.

Vibrato A performing technique where the pitch of a note slightly wavers to give the sound greater warmth and resonance.

Wah-wah mute An effect when a brass player alternately applies and removes a mute; on an electric guitar when the player controls output from the amplifier with a pedal.

Walking bass Common in both Baroque music and 20th century jazz and blues, a bass part with a regular rhythm throughout a piece, akin to feet walking.

Whole-tone scale A scale where there is a whole tone between all the notes, with no semitones as there would be in a conventional scale.

Word painting Music written to reflect the meaning of the words, e.g. ascending when the words mention climbing a mountain.

Acknowledgements:

From Both Sides Now
Words and music by Joni Mitchell. © Copyright 1967 Siquomb Publishing Corp. Westminster Music Limited. All Rights Reserved. International Copyright Secured.

The Gun Barrel Battle (From 'Lost Odyssey')
Music by Nobuo Uematsu. © Copyright 2007 Aniplex Incorporated. Sony/ATV Music Publishing. All Rights Reserved. International Copyright Secured.

I Cain't Say No (From 'Oklahoma!')
Words by Oscar Hammerstein II, music by Richard Rodgers. © Copyright 1943 & 1955 Williamson Music Company, USA. Copyright Renewed. Williamson Music Company owner of publication and allied rights for all countries of the Western Hemisphere and Japan. Williamson Music Limited for all countries of the Eastern Hemisphere (except Japan). Print Rights administered by Hal Leonard LLC. All Rights Reserved. International Copyright Secured.